VOICES FROM THE NATIONS

We the

Russians

VOICES FROM THE NATIONS

WE THE CHINESE: *Voices from China* edited by Deirdre and Neale Hunter

WE THE VIETNAMESE: *Voices from Vietnam* edited by François Sully

WE THE BURMESE: *Voices from Burma* edited by Helen G. Trager

WE THE RUSSIANS

Voices from Russia

Edited by Colette Shulman

PRAEGER PUBLISHERS

New York · Washington · London

PRAEGER PUBLISHERS
111 Fourth Avenue, New York, N.Y. 10003, U.S.A.
5, Cromwell Place, London S.W.7, England

Published in the United States of America in 1971
by Praeger Publishers, Inc.

Second printing, 1972

© 1971 by Praeger Publishers, Inc.

Library of Congress Catalog Card Number: 78–83345

Printed in the United States of America

CONTENTS

List of Illustrations   ix

Preface   xi

Acknowledgments   xiv

PART ONE: *Exodus from the Village*

A BOYHOOD RECALLED   3

SOME HARD SIDES OF VILLAGE LIFE   9

THE URGE TO EXPLORE   15

THE "BRAIN DRAIN" AND SUGGESTIONS FOR REFORM ON
    THE FARM: TWO VIEWS   19

CULTURAL FACILITIES IN WESTERN SIBERIA   27

ZINA'S CLUB   31

POLITICAL EDUCATION ON A FARM   37

LETTER FROM A GRANDMOTHER   40

PART TWO: *Conversations with and About Young People in the City*

FOUR HIGH SCHOOL STUDENTS TRY OUT THEIR ENGLISH   45

SPEAKING FREELY—MASHA, YURI, AND ZOYA   52
LOOKING BEYOND ONESELF: TWO VIEWS   63
A WRITER REFLECTS   65

PART THREE: *Attitudes Toward Material Things*

A GIRL WRESTLES WITH A PROBLEM   73
TONYECHKA (A SONG)   76
SOME YOUNG PEOPLE'S GOALS   78
ARE SOME PARENTS OVERDOING IT?   80
THE MATERIAL SIDE OF UNIVERSITY LIFE   85

PART FOUR: *Scenes from the Life of a Young Worker*

1. THE USUAL   92
2. CHERNYSHEV CLOSE UP   95
3. ON THE STREET CORNER   101
4. RELATIVES   103
5. CHATTER   106
6. CHERNYSHEV'S AUTOBIOGRAPHY   108
7. BEGINNING A NEW LIFE   112
8. A LETTER TO PETER   114

PART FIVE: *Feeling for the Land and the Culture*

"A FEAST OF ROWANBERRIES"   118
A WALK IN DOSTOYEVSKY'S CITY   123
A SMALL CULTURAL OUTPOST IN SIBERIA   129
ALONG THE ROAD   130
A WORKING SUMMER ON THE ISLANDS UP NORTH   137
"OLD RUSSIA HAS BECOME FASHIONABLE"   142
THE TRADITIONS OF PEASANT WEDDINGS   148
AN UNSENTIMENTAL VIEW   156

PART SIX: *Manners and Morals*

"LONG LIVE COURTEOUS MEN!" 161
THE COMPLICATED QUESTION OF MODERN MANNERS 163
FIFTEEN BOYS 170
HOW FAR SHOULD A GIRL GO? 172
MARINA GETS A LECTURE 177
PREPARATION FOR THE KINGDOM OF LOVE 181
UNINFORMED OPINIONS 183
TWO YOUNG MARRIAGES 186

PART SEVEN: *Pacifism, Patriotism, and War*

I AM GOYA 199
"WHY SHOULD WE FIGHT WITH AMERICA?" 200
THE DOVE AND THE OLIVE BRANCH, OR THE HAMMER
    AND SICKLE? 202
A FOURTEEN-YEAR-OLD IN SVERDLOVSK 204
FROM WAR LITERATURE 206
WHAT THE MILITARY MEN SAY 213
THE WHOLE TRUTH 216
LOW-KEYED LOYALTY 218
THEY LOVED LEMONADE 223

PART EIGHT: *Officially Sponsored Criticism and Voices of Dissent*
Officially Sponsored Criticism

ON CATCHING UP WITH THE CAPITALISTS 228
WHO IS TO BLAME? 230
SVETLANA'S CULTURAL PITCH 233
"THANK YOU, COMRADE PROFESSOR" 236
THE TATTOOED POEM 240
A KIND OF ALIENATION 243

Voices of Dissent

ASK, BOYS!   244
FEELING ISOLATED   246
CASES FROM THE "CHRONICLE"   248
BUKOVSKY'S STATEMENT   252
THE KGB TALKS WITH LITVINOV   259
A LETTER FROM TWENTY-FOUR STUDENTS   262
BACKLASH   264
THE DUTY OF A COMMUNIST   267

PART NINE: *Jobs and Ambitions*

RUSSIAN HORATIO ALGERS   271
A WOMAN CONSTRUCTION WORKER   275
WHO WILL DO THE UNPOPULAR JOBS?   278
WHO GOES TO THE UNIVERSITY?: SOME STATISTICS FROM
    GORKY   280
WHAT ARE THE SCHOOLS PREPARING PEOPLE FOR?   282
CHOOSING A PROFESSION   286
"YOU COULD HAVE BECOME AN ENGINEER"   291

Glossary   295
Suggestions for Further Reading   298
Index   299

LIST OF ILLUSTRATIONS

Village	xvi
Farm girls	10
Harvesting potatoes	13
"Sitting pretty"	24
"Burning his bridges"	30
Moscow park	44
The "Metelitsa" cafe	55
Informal classroom	58
More traditional classroom	68
An English-language school	69
Krokodil, No. 1, 1969	70
Window shopping	83
Young workers	97
Dancing in a cafe	107
Moscow winter	116
Summer in the countryside	134
Students at work in the Solovetsky Islands	138
Old Russia: village and birches	144
Old Bratsk	155
New Bratsk	155
A disapproving stare	158
Sun, Air, and Water	184

First-graders in Red Square   205
Youngsters at a war memorial   205
A live-statue tableau   215
Winners in a war-game competition   217
Workers in Bratsk   238
High school students   268
Waiting to take examinations at Moscow University   281
Vocational training   284
Young people at a construction site, Siberia   293

No generalization can be wholly fair about life in Russia. The complexity of the Soviet system defies a single snapshot. The country has Establishment people, anti-Establishment people, and a great many who are neither. There are those whose ambitions and drives are channeled in officially approved ways and others who find their fulfillment in the private crevices of the society. What this book tries to do is give a sampling of a number of different aspects of Russian life. It tries to convey to the reader a sense of what life would be like for him if he had been born in the Soviet Union.

Nevertheless, if I had to single out one general impression, it would be that this is a country in transition from a predominantly agricultural village life to one that is more and more industrial, and this fact has been the basic shaping force in the lives of most of its people, especially the young.

The way to approach the country, it seems to me, is to look at the process of change—to ask not only what is Soviet society like now, but where is it moving, what is it becoming? Since my first visit to Moscow in 1955, there have been some visible changes, and much more has happened under the surface and inside people's minds that can be felt in new attitudes and values. Contact with the outside world has become more commonplace. The most evident sign of this is the speed with which fads and fashions of dress and music from other parts of the world appear in Moscow, Leningrad, and other Soviet cities. Women's attitudes toward their role in the society are clearly undergoing revision, and young people seem far less inclined than their parents were to accept unquestioningly the goals and models held up to them by authority. Does this mean that political attitudes are changing as well? Here I must register the impression that changes in the rest of the society are extremely slow to find reflection in the political realm. The whole system works to reinforce in the minds of Soviet citizens a fundamental Communist view, which is also traditionally Russian, that the leadership knows better than the people what is in their best interests. In the years since Khrushchev's ouster, the trend has been toward more strictness and rigidity in ideology rather than toward relaxation. But even if change is not always toward liberalization, it at least reflects movement and ferment—people thinking, people questioning and searching. I have tried to select materials that convey the yeasty spirit of the Russians, their natural warmth and ebullience, which give Russian life an intensity seldom encountered in other places, and which seem to heighten the contrast between the good and the bad in their society. Despite the barriers to the outside world, the essential spirit that animates people elsewhere manages to communicate itself to the Russian people and is most strongly felt by the young. This reminds a visitor to Moscow that regardless of differences in system, ideology, and culture, there is a fundamental unity of men everywhere.

This book makes no effort to cover the non-Russian peoples of the Soviet Union—the Baltic nationalities, those of the Caucasus and Central Asia, the Ukrainians, the Moldavians, and numerous other national groups throughout the country. The Soviet people are very much aware of their particular nationalities. Their cultures vary greatly, and there are important differences in their attitudes. It would be impossible within the scope of these pages to do justice to this enormous heterogeneity. However, many of the views expressed in this book (largely, but not exclusively, by Russians) are widely held views shared by Soviet peoples of many nationalities.

The materials used here come from three kinds of sources: books, newspapers, and magazines published legally in the Soviet Union; the underground Soviet press; and oral conversations. Most of the material is excerpted from the original Russian-language sources. In the interests of readability, signs indicating the numerous excisions have not been placed in the text, but an effort has been made to preserve the sense of the original.

I wish to thank the School of International Affairs at Columbia University, whose facilities have assisted me greatly. I also wish to thank Mary Mackler for her wise and generous help and Peter Reddaway for permission to use his translation from *The Chronicle* on pp. 248–51. I express my appreciation to Dr. Richard Eustis of Hancock, New Hampshire, for giving me access to the tranquil environment of the Hancock Town Library in its off-hours. Somehow the writing always goes better up there. This, incidentally, may be the only U. S. library whose front door key unintentionally traveled all the way to Moscow and back.

February, 1971

ACKNOWLEDGMENTS

The editor gratefully acknowledges permission to reprint numerous excerpts from articles translated in *The Current Digest of the Soviet Press*, an invaluable source of current Soviet material, published weekly at Ohio State University, Columbus, Ohio, by the American Association for the Advancement of Slavic Studies. All translations copyright in the year of their publication by *The Current Digest of the Soviet Press*. They are:

Literary Gazette, July 26, 1966, from Vol. XVIII, No. 33, 1966, in "Some Hard Sides of Village Life."

Literary Gazette, July 23 and July 26, 1966, from Vol. XVIII, No. 33, 1966, in "The Urge to Explore."

Literary Gazette, December 27, 1967, from Vol. XX, No. 2, 1968, and *Literary Gazette*, February 7, 1968, from Vol. XX, No. 8, 1968, both in "The 'Brain Drain' and Suggestions for Reform."

Pravda, June 19, 1969, from Vol. XXI, No. 25, 1969, and *Pravda*, January 22, 1967, from Vol. XIX, No. 3, 1967, both in "Are Some Parents Overdoing It?."

Komsomolskaya pravda, December 8, 15, and 29, 1967, from Vol. XIX, No. 7, 1967, in "The Complicated Question of Modern Manners."

Pravda, November 18, 1968, from Vol. XX, No. 46, 1968, in "Preparation for the Kingdom of Love."

Yunost, No. 3, 1968, from Vol. XX, No. 15, 1968, in "Uninformed Opinions."

Red Star, February 9, 1964, from Vol. XVI, No. 5, 1964, and *Red Star*, March 27, 1969, from Vol. XXI, No. 13, 1969, in "What the Military Men Say."

Komsomolskaya pravda, June 3, 1967, from Vol. XIX, No. 26, 1967, in "Svetlana's Cultural Pitch."

In addition, the editor acknowledges permission to reprint the following:

Excerpt in "The 'Brain Drain' and Suggestions for Reform" and "Political Education on a Farm," from *Involuntary Journey to Siberia*, by Andrei Amalrik, translated by Manya Harari and Max Hayward (New York: Harcourt Brace Jovanovich, 1970). By permission of Harcourt Brace Jovanovich.

"A Small Cultural Outpost in Siberia," from *The Endless Steppe: Growing Up in Siberia*, by Esther Hautzig (New York: Thomas Y. Crowell Company, 1968). © 1968 by Esther Hautzig, by permission of Thomas Y. Crowell Company.

"Along the Road," from *Going to Town and Other Stories*, by Yuri Kazakov, compiled and translated by Gabriella Azrael (Boston: Houghton Mifflin Company, 1964). By permission of Houghton Mifflin Company.

"Fifteen Boys," from *The New Russian Poets, 1953 to 1966*, selected, edited, and translated by George Reavey (New York: October House, 1966). © 1966, 1968 by George Reavey, by permission of October House.

"I Am Goya," from *Antiworlds and "The Fifth Ace," Poetry by Andrei Voznesensky*, edited by Patricia Blake and Max Hayward (New York: Anchor Books, Doubleday and Company, 1967). By permission of Doubleday and Company.

"The Tattooed Poem," translated in *Atlas Magazine*, March, 1969. By permission of *Atlas Magazine*.

A characteristic village, combining new and old buildings   (*Novosti*)

PART ONE

Exodus from the Village

Western travelers to the Soviet Union hardly ever
get out of the cities and into the real countryside
—a land so unbelievably vast that it sweeps from
Central Europe to the easternmost point in Asia
and from the frozen tundra to the tropical deserts
where nomads roam. All across this vastness are
the villages and farmsteads of Russia, more than
half a million of them, "scattered like peas over
the expanses of our land," as one writer put it.
Imagine what it is like to grow up in one of those
villages, deep in the northern woods or out on
the central steppe: the rugged winters to contend
with, the dirt roads that are impassable for much
of the year, the sense of being so far from everything—a feeling that grows more intense as television extends its reach into the remote areas and
the newspapers bring reports of big happenings
around the country. It was inevitable that the
venturesome and the restless among the village
young would try and get away to become part
of the country's drive for industrialization. They
have been migrating to the cities at a rate that is
faster than almost anywhere else in the world, to
the point where the migration has aroused con-

cern about the conditions of life in the village. Even in Moscow, most of the people you see are at best just a generation away from the country-side, and the culture they reflect is still in many ways a peasant one.

A BOYHOOD RECALLED

*Vladimir Soloukhin, a poet and essayist from the
Vladimir region northeast of Moscow, writes
about his boyhood in the village in the late
1930's. The rowdy doings he tells of could just
as well describe growing up in the countryside
today, but what was different then, and poignant,
was the way World War II yanked those boys
out of their own small world and changed their
lives for good. This is part of a story entitled
"The Grievance," which appeared in translation
in the magazine* Soviet Literature, No. 2, 1963.

The village of Cherkutino used to be a trading center,
with fairs on Saint Peter's Day, at Shrovetide, and on other
high holidays to which the peasants would come from all the
surrounding countryside. And though it had long since lost
its significance as a central market place, it was still the
focus for the region, and our school was there.

We kids from Vishenki, from Olino, from Volkhovo, from
Pasynkovo, from twenty or even twenty-five villages around,
all attended the fifth to seventh grades in Cherkutino.

We'd get up before dawn (it was a three-mile walk from
Olepino), wait for each other at the crossroads, and then
trudge off, the whole bunch of us from Olepino, together.

As we approached we could see in the early morning violet
haze lines of dark figures moving towards Cherkutino from

all directions and would try to make out who was who: those were the kids from Burdachovo, those over there were from Kudelino.

At school I shared a desk with Kolya Lantsev, who lived in Kudelino. Kolya had a round, freckled face with fair, tender skin, the kind that bruised easily. Of the two of us, Kolya was unquestionably the more mischievous. He was always getting into fights. During every recess he'd tangle either with Mishka Sadovnikov from Snegiryovo or with Vanka Zheryakov from Zelnyaki. During class, when he couldn't very well fight, he would roll ink-balls and throw them at the girls or take a stick and nudge the elbow of the boy sitting in front doing his writing exercises.

As for me, more often than not I was reading a book during class.

They say a person is known by the company he keeps, meaning, usually, bad company. Take two boys who are friends. If one smokes and the other doesn't, it's generally assumed that the boy who smokes is not going to stop smoking, and the one who doesn't will inevitably start. With Kolya and me it was the other way around. Of course, reading storybooks in class is not a great virtue, but it is better than throwing ink-balls.

It began when Kolya pulled my book out of my hands just for the fun of it. I couldn't start a tussle then and there, so I had to keep still, though I was good and angry. Kolya automatically looked down at the open page, read a couple of sentences, then the page, and then read steadily till the end of the class.

Books evidently opened up an entirely new world to him, a very different world from Kudelino and Cherkutino, with their inevitable brawls on feast days, or from an algebra lesson.

Now Kolya no longer spent the recesses getting into fights. Oblivious of everything, sometimes even of nature's call, he would keep company with the mammoths, feeding them sweet shoots, or sit by a bonfire with Dersu Uzala, or sail down the Mississippi with Huckleberry Finn. We finished the seventh grade and parted good friends, but afterward, of course, we hardly ever saw each other, except sometimes at the holiday merrymaking in Cherkutino.

But then, just before the war, we met under the following circumstances. We, that is, my crowd, were in our mid-teens by then, nearly grown youths.

One day the fellows from Kudelino showed up in Olepino for the Saturday night merrymaking. This was sheer provocation. There was a standing feud between Olepino and the Vorsha, that is, the villages along the Vorsha River, and Kudelino had always been the Vorsha ringleader. Now the Vorsha gang had just walked into our midst!

True, they had come with peaceful aims, socially, so to speak. But everybody knew that our Shurka Moskovsky of Olepino and Sashka Matveyev of Kudelino each had an eye on the same girl, and that meant there wouldn't be enough room for both of them. And once the older fellows decided to fight, we younger ones hadn't a chance to keep out of it.

Shurka signaled us to meet him a little way off and whispered his instructions to us.

"We're gonna beat the daylights out of the Kudelino gang tonight," he said. "We'll join in the fun for a while, act as if there's nothing wrong. Mind you, don't give a sign. When Ivan Mitrich starts ringing the bell for twelve o'clock, we'll go after them. I'll go straight for Sashka Matveyev. He's a big fellow, so you'll help me, Yurka. You'll take on Vanka Lysy, Vaska; Vitka, you'll take Kolka Sofronov. Valka and Borka'll take Vaska Zelnikovsky, and you (here our chief pointed to me) will take Kolya Lantsev. That's the way we'll start. We'll plan the rest as we go along. Now everybody go home and get big sticks. We'll hide them underneath the school porch. . . .

I tried to keep out of sight of my "customer" but still near him, the better to be able to carry out my assignment when midnight struck. But Kolya recognized me, even though it was dark, and started talking to me. It would have been better if he had picked on me or cursed me, or if we'd quarreled over something. The changeover would not have had to be so sudden. Here we are talking and laughing and then, bang!—a sock on the jaw!

To make things worse, Kolya said he was thirsty, and I had to take him to my house for a drink of cold water from the Kunin well. All the way there I wondered what I should do if the signal came en route: should I fight Kolya in single combat or detain him and let the rumpus take place without us.

Then something completely unexpected happened. At about half-past eleven Sashka Matveyev gave a piercing whistle and the enemy, one and all, detached themselves from the gay crowd and started for home in a body. Five minutes later, we heard fifteen strident voices singing:

> Through the village we walk, singing,
> From end to end, from left to right.
> If in the barn the girls are sleeping
> We'll ask if we can spend the night.

The unforeseen departure caused some confusion in our ranks. But Shurka Moskovsky would never be at peace if things had ended so tamely.

"Come on, fellows, grab your sticks and let's go after them! We'll catch up with them at the ravine. Follow me!"

In the haste and the darkness I got hold of a light, dried-up stick. This bothered me no end. Since I had to go into battle I wanted to have a reliable weapon.

As we neared the enemy we gave our battle cry, that is, we yelled blasphemies and shouted, "Kill Kudelino!"—to which the Kudelino gang reacted by taking to their heels.

This added fuel to our fires, and we ran faster. The chase ended when we reached the last house in the village, where a wide meadow began. The Kudelino crowd knew what they were about. They had brought stout cudgels with them from Kudelino and hidden them on the outskirts of the village. Now they grabbed their weapons and turned to face us with closed ranks. . . .

In this kind of fight the main assault never lasts long. You hit someone, someone hits you, then it is all over.

My dry stick broke in two at the first blow, leaving me with a useless stub. At the same moment my head buzzed and everything turned dark, my teeth chattered and my ears felt stuffed with cotton wool. Someone had hit me back. Through a haze I saw a figure in front of me with a stick. I flung myself upon it and grabbed hold of the stick with both hands. My face nearly touched that of the lucky owner of the stick. It was Kolya Lantsev. As he struggled to break my hold he was struck from two sides. He swayed, straightened up, then turned and fled. The others followed suit.

We returned to the village in a fever of triumph.

Generally speaking, this was an ordinary village fight and quickly forgotten. Besides, the war broke out soon after and all the lads were called up. The majority of them never returned to the banks of the sparkling little Vorsha River.

Four years of war. Why, even four ordinary years spent away from home would have seemed like an eternity, and those were war years. Besides, my pals and I were barely eighteen when we left our villages. The world we found ourselves in was so different from anything we had ever known, the days and even the hours so eventful as to be equal to several years of normal living; toward the end of my fourth year in the army, believe it or not, I had begun to forget the names of some of the villages in my district. When I think of it now I can hardly believe it myself, but it is a fact. I remember it well. Once I tried to recall the names of the villages on the Vorsha and couldn't think of Kuryanikha and Demikhovo. Everything that had happened to us in our childhood and boyhood, in fact, everything that had happened to us before the war, seemed to have been in another life, not ours, not on this earth.

SOME HARD SIDES

OF VILLAGE LIFE

Here are some flash glimpses of conditions that drove many peasants and urban-educated specialists away from the village in the first years after the war, on through the 1950's and into the 1960's, when, toward the end of the decade, the living standard on the farms really began to improve.

My mama lived her whole life in the village. But she wanted her sons' lot to be different from hers. She was always threatening us that if we did badly in our studies we would have to "go to work on the collective farm" or "become a herdsman." I was afraid of the collective farm, because it meant a straw roof full of holes on the cowshed, a farm chairman who was a drunkard, an almost illiterate stableman who could only read the signboard above the store, and a calculating night watchman, Uncle Grisha, who believed that "doktrina Eizenhauera" [the "Eisenhower Doctrine"] was the President's daughter.

Selskaya molodezh (Village Youth),
No. 9, 1967

I had visited the village of Lyapino when it was an independent collective farm—that was about fifteen years ago

Some girls who did not leave   (*Novosti*)

[1954]. The village was such a backwater that I had to walk
the last ten kilometers; the district committee's car couldn't
get through the mud. I was on my first journalistic mission, a
newspaper correspondent investigating a letter. The school-
girl's letter, written in an immature, childish hand on a sheet
of paper torn out of a copybook, told of horrible things. It
said that the collective farm chairman beat the collective
farmers. I remember staring at the chairman in surprise—he
was a haggard-looking man in felt boots with rubber soles,
which he wore even in the summer—and listening to his complaints about his health and to his angry mutterings: "You've
got to keep a tight rein on the people," and, "You've got to
keep the bit on the people."

Selskaya molodezh, No. 2, 1969

All together, there were seventeen of us first cousins at that
wedding in our native village of Manylovitsa. The family

statistics provide food for thought: Of the seventeen, all of whom are the same age and grew to adulthood in the years immediately following the war, only one had been married in our native village.

Adolf Rieder, the Totma District Party secretary, told me that in 1940 the number of persons working on the collective farms of the district was 16,796, whereas in 1967 it was only 4,000! What is the reason for the decline? Is it the low incomes and unpaid labor? Certainly that was why my cousins left the village after the war. They wanted to make a living and were looking for a dependable crust of bread for themselves and their families somewhere else.

Selskaya molodezh, No. 2, 1969

By the beginning of the 1950's, the collective farms of Smolensk Province could as a rule ensure the peasant neither bread nor money. Overtaxation of the peasant household was another source of trouble. Each able-bodied member of the family, especially if single, was a source of taxes; is it surprising that his family should try to get rid of him?

By no means every household, moreover, had anything to sell in order to pay those taxes. Some families had to have help from the city, had to have someone there to send a little real money now and then. In 1950, therefore, eighteen young men left a village of fifteen households to go to trade school in Moscow together.

That may be the way the tradition of leaving for the city came into being. It is possible, too, that the well-known arbitrary limitations set on personal plots at the beginning of the 1960's precipitated the second wave of migration that undermined the stabilization, and even a numerical growth, of rural young people that had been observed since 1955.

Literaturnaya gazeta (Literary Gazette), July 26, 1966

I am telling you not a parable but a true story. As much as possible I will tell it in the words of its organizer and central figure—let us call him the "Man of Action"—who ten years ago, no longer young, went to work for three years in a Voronezh village in the most remote part of the backwoods. To work as the school director.

When he arrived, he was horrified. Thirteen years after the end of the war there was not a single sapling growing in this village—its ground was full of shell cases and burned-out flame-throwers. Some families still lived in dugouts. There was no bathhouse in the village, and the children had lice. The teachers were all local women who had not finished high school, and in dress and manner they looked like ordinary peasants. When they got together at recess time, the talk was about the latest litter of pigs and fodder for the winter— and nothing else. There was no discipline whatsoever. Even the cleaning women had become so lazy that they just threw the contents of their slop pails right outside the front door, so that you could get into the school only by climbing over an impressive mountain of icy garbage.

Alas, one had to begin with these humdrum things.

They took away eighty-two truckloads of garbage before they had cleared the entrance to the school, garbage in its natural state. As for the garbage of cloddishness, coarseness, stupidity, and indifference, which was enough to make you want to scream—to howl like a wolf—in what units does one measure that?

Yunost (Youth), No. 7, 1967

At the end of last year [1966], the Voronezh newspaper *Young Communard* published a letter without return address under the pompous headline "I'll Leave the Village Anyway!"

"Don't throw any of your village lyricism at me: the dawn and the quiet pools in the river and the sunsets. I have a

Harvesting potatoes: Much of the field work is done by women. (*Novosti*)

feeling and a love for all this no less than some of the 'village' poets do.

"And don't reproach me for arrogance and disrespect toward the people of the village—I saw and know very well how they work and earn their bread.

"Both the first lesson and the classroom routine excite me. I love my work as a teacher; I love my pupils and enjoy teaching them. But this passes, and the force of habit soon takes over. There is the rain for days on end without stopping, the mud and heavy boots, and the cluster of drunken men at the store. In essence, I have been lonely all these three years—let my colleagues not take offense; they are older than I and wiser in the experience of life; they are totally satisfied by their work and concerns about their household affairs.

"I want to have day-to-day personal contact with people who are close to me in spirit and ways of thinking. These people are in the city. I hear conversations—about the Taganka Theater, the letters of Van Gogh, a book of Martynov's poems that is just out, a new poet. And I have a horrible feeling that such conversations are over my head. I don't want to stagnate mentally and spiritually, yet I sense that this irreversible and terrible process has already begun in me."

Yunost, No. 7, 1967

The peasants' standard of living is going up. Statistics testify to this: In 1967, the collective farmers of Totma District, like those of the rest of Vologda Province, were paid an average of 2.8 rubles for a workday (in 1964 they received 1.64 rubles). What this means to the collective farmers can be seen from the figures for, say, the very average Bolshevik Collective Farm, where the rate of pay was eighteen kopeks below the district average. On that collective farm, average monthly earnings were 105 to 107 rubles for milkmaids, 85 to 86 rubles for tractor drivers, 88 rubles for truck drivers, and 45 to 46 rubles for people in the field brigades. Considering that every family has its kitchen garden and that most families have their own milk, eggs, and meat, it cannot be said that the peasants of a very average collective farm live badly. And so they have begun to build new houses, celebrate holidays, and buy motorcycles, furniture, and clothes.

We used to think that when things got straightened out on the collective farms, the young people would no longer be eager to get away from them and go to the city. Now that time is upon us, yet the young people do not remain in the villages.

Selskaya molodezh (*Village Youth*),
No. 2, 1969

THE URGE TO EXPLORE

Village boys love to be around machines and engines of all kinds, and they seek the skills needed to operate them. For many, the search for training is the first step toward leaving home. Some go with no intention of returning, while others just drift away gradually—as you can see from the selections that follow. In the first piece, a nineteen-year-old lad speaks of the powerful inner drives that lead him to explore other worlds; in the second, a writer takes a look at such boys and sketches the pattern of their migration; and in the third, the same writer shows what happens to some of the girls when the boys leave.

Hello, Dear Editors of *Yunost!*

I work as a boatswain on a freighter that sails the Dnieper, the Desna, and the Pripyat. I am nineteen years old.

When I was in Chernigov not long ago, I bought a copy of your magazine and found it very interesting. Here's what I want to tell you. For several years now, every boy and girl in our town has spent a month or two weeks of summer vacation working on a collective farm or a state farm. And this is the way it ought to be. From the time we were in school, we have been used to working in the fields and to working in general.

After graduating from eighth grade, most of us went to work on a state farm. At fifteen I already had a tractor driver's license, at sixteen I was a certified electrician, and at seventeen I was testing new tractors. And now I am a boatswain on a ship.

I have tried to keep on learning and to experience everything for myself. And so are all young people drawn to new things and to the unknown. But often older people have no confidence in us.

Here is an example. A boy graduates from the eighth grade and wants to go to work in a sawmill, let's say. They tell him, "You're still young, you'll break something and make a mess of things, and we'll have to answer for it." With their distrust, grownups frighten away the young people, who get the feeling they are good for nothing.

The more young people are trusted in our country, the more young skilled personnel we will have. I myself am very young and more than once have felt all this distrust and disesteem of the young directed at me. Yet I managed to get what I wanted. How did I do it? I went to the head office of the farm to see if they would send me to a machine-operators' course. They asked me how old I was. I knew you had to be at least fifteen and a half to get into the course, so that's how old I said I was. They took me at my word without asking for identification and gave me the papers I needed to get into the course. That's how I got to study and, later on, to work, and I found the work interesting. Then I learned some other trades before becoming a boatswain.

I like being a boatswain, because here in the merchant marine at least they don't treat me like a child who is still too young and is to be distrusted for fear he will make a mess of things. They have an unwritten law here—once you've become a seaman you have to work on the same level as everyone else; there's no allowance made for youth. I like this. Sometimes it happens that we work twenty-four hours straight without sleep, and even forty-eight hours. And nobody tells me to go to bed. This I like too. I feel in seventh heaven, because these people have confidence in me, they believe I can work on an equal level with them and can go without sleep for as long as they can.

But I don't want to stay in this job forever. I would give a lot if I could just once fly the YAK-18 training plane by myself. This has been a persistent dream of mine ever since my school days. Don't think it's a child's foolish fancy. It is the reason why I became a tractor driver after graduating from eighth grade—to feel in control of an engine. It is why I became an electrician—to experiment with heights. But those heights turned out to be too low, and there was no risk at all up there. I love to take risks, I love height and speed. And you know yourself what the speed of a tractor is.

Engines have a powerful attraction for me. I love machines and I would give anything just to be at the wheel of a ship, to feel the tension of a spring and of levers, to drive a car, and to fly an airplane.

So long, comrades. A seaman's greeting to you.—Vasili G.

The *Dnepropetrovsk*, Port of Amur
Yunost (Youth), No. 2, 1968

Let us assume that a boy has passed through eight grades of schooling and is not tempted by the laurels of an Academician but wants to stay in his native village and raise grain. However, even if he is sixteen, he may not, according to our labor legislation, be put behind the wheel of a tractor. To go to school he must be sent to the city, and he begins to lead a life in two places. Buying thirty-five kopeks' worth of pretzels on Saturday, he sets out for home; on Monday he returns on the crowded bus to his dormitory, laden with food packages from the village.

Let us assume that he has withstood the temptations of the city, has come home and taken his place behind the wheel and has completed the duties expected of a novice. During his second year, when he might really be expected to be an asset to the farm, he goes off to the army. When he has finished his military service, he will take a job on a construction site (for his service-acquired trade, happily, is in demand everywhere), or will marry a city girl, or will be won over by his comrades, or will "come to his senses" by himself —but he will never return to his native village, for he has been sliced cleanly away from Smolensk Province. And once the young men have gone, the young women are sure to follow; they are not disposed simply to wither away on the vine. Through the force of objective circumstances, through distortion of the sexual balance, we have simply been "driving" the girls from the countryside.

Literaturnaya gazeta (Literary Gazette), July 23, 1966

The production-training school of the Smolensk Meat-Packing Combine has been monopolized by girls from the countryside. Only five of its hundred trainees originally came from the city. Their work is hard and comparatively low-paid. In the poultry-processing shop, saturated with the odor of blood, the girls finish plucking the dead but still quivering chickens by hand. The place is damp and untidy. We asked the girls if they were aware that—in addition to the healthy country air, the blue skies, and being with their mothers—they would earn about twice as much in the dairy sections of their farms as they were earning in the city, besides which they would not have to live in cubicles rented from lonely old ladies.

No, they hadn't been aware of this.

Literaturnaya gazeta, July 26, 1966

THE "BRAIN DRAIN" AND

SUGGESTIONS FOR REFORM

ON THE FARM:

TWO VIEWS

Many Soviet journalists, by bringing to light the conditions in the countryside, have been trying to point the way toward solutions of age-old peasant problems. They are sociologists of a sort, and polemicists as well. One of them is Alexander Yanov, who has been studying the migration of young people. Here are parts of his article published in Literaturnaya gazeta *(Literary Gazette) on December 27, 1967.*

Many prescriptions have already been suggested for treating this "disease" [migration]. Mention has been made of building clubhouses for young people, improving housing construction in the countryside, increasing people's material well-being, and so forth.

Undeniably, all this is important. But alas, practice has irrefutably shown that none of these measures actually works when taken separately, apart from the entire context of present-day social, political, and cultural problems. Educated rural young people are leaving the clubhouses, the housing, the prosperous life. Apparently plenty to eat, a roof over their heads, and dancing in the clubhouse are not enough for them.

There is no such thing as a single process of migration of young people from the countryside! There are three different streams, rooted in different social phenomena. Consequently, different measures are required to regulate them.

The first stream, in point of size, comprises school "dropouts," youngsters who for one reason or another have not completed eight years of schooling. Strange as it may seem, there are quite a few such youngsters in the countryside. This stream heads for the city to work—at construction projects, at meat-packing or linen combines, in short, at jobs that young city people find rather unattractive.

The second stream is recruited from the fourteen- and fifteen-year-olds who have completed the eighth grade but who at that age are still entirely unprepared to choose their future paths independently. However, their parents are quite well prepared to do it for them—and rural youngsters fill the countless craft and factory training schools in the cities, constituting the main contingents in these schools. The "motor" of the second stream is parental will and insistence, which are themselves the consequence of the greatly declined prestige of agricultural labor in recent years and of the persistent stereotype that has taken shape in the peasants' minds: We want our children to live differently. Since this second stream has its roots not so much in the minds of the teenagers as in the minds of their parents, it can be only partially influenced by material incentives alone.

And, finally, there is the third stream of migration, the smallest but the one that plays the part of, to use Chernyshevsky's words, "the caffeine in the tea, the bouquet in a fine wine"—the graduates of secondary schools. And almost all of them, who could really become the "motor of motors" of rural society, its real transformers, leave the countryside. They go away, never to return. Even if they become specialists in

agricultural production. Everyone is familiar with the lament-
able statistics on the number of specialists who "strike roots"
in the countryside. As a result, more than 90 per cent of
middle management personnel, those in direct charge of
production on our collective farms, have had only an
elementary education.

The Andreyev Collective Farm has twelve brigade leaders
and assistants. And how many of these, do you think, are
young people? Not a single one. How many of them, do you
think, have had at least eight years of schooling? Not a single
one! The situation is the same at the Michurin State Farm.
There are no young people, there are no educated people in
responsible positions. Moreover, just take a look at the composition of the collective farm board. In both 1964 and 1966,
ten of the thirteen members had had only an elementary education, and only two were under thirty. In effect, educated
young people here do not participate in the management of
their farm, their society. And perhaps this is why there is no
scope in the countryside for their intellectual and creative
powers. And these powers are rebelling.

> Yanov then discusses two reforms that were tried out on a few
> farms in the middle and late 1960's in an effort to slow down
> migration. The Kostroma experiment, named after the region
> where it took place, involved paying young people higher wages
> than they could expect to receive in the city—in effect, creating
> privileges for them. In the other experiment, special mechanized
> teams were set up on a farm and "attached" to particular areas
> of land, that is, given responsibility over them through all of the
> seasonal phases from sowing to harvesting. Yanov says those
> experiments were definitely in the right direction but goes on
> to tell why he believes they could never be really effective unless
> accompanied by broader changes of a social and political nature
> in the village.

For it is clear that both the Kostroma experiment and the
organization of labor by teams both have the same roots;

they are both symptoms of the same in-depth experimental quest for new forms of social ties among people, for new forms and methods of attracting people to labor, which V. I. Lenin spoke of as a natural law of our society.

And both these undertakings have stopped halfway, have fallen short of completion, have failed to manifest even a small fraction of their enormous potential. Both have come up against the stone wall of the administrative structure of rural society.

Let us look at that structure in greater detail. For the sake of brevity I shall resort to a comparison. The ceiling begins to leak in your city apartment. Or your neighborhood store has run out of milk. Or you need a taxi. Do you take all these problems to your boss? On collective farms that would be standard procedure. If you have to order milk for your children from the warehouse, get a delivery of peat or firewood, build or repair your house, or procure cornstalks—and what might not a villager need?—you cannot bypass the collective farm chairman. There is a duality in his role in rural society; he performs two entirely different functions in it. He is two persons, as it were, the organizer of production and the leader of the community. After all, the person who has in his hands the building materials, fuel, fodder for privately owned livestock and, most important in rural areas, transportation also has concentrated in his hands the predominant social influence, in other words, the real power. Of course, rural society has at its disposal many democratic institutions—the general membership meeting, the village Soviet, the Party organization and, finally, the collective farm board. But if you are in desperate need of a truck or milk or some other extremely vital material necessity this very day, you cannot wait for a membership meeting, nor would you go to the village Soviet, which does not deal with the things you need for the simple reason that it does not have them at its disposal. In real life all roads lead to Rome, as the saying goes, or to the chairman of the collective farm board. Now let us take a look at the composition of the board.

Who is on it, who is called upon not only to lead but also to exercise control—between meetings, for two whole years— over the entire farm management and all the activities of its leadership? Seven-tenths of the Andreyev board is made up of the officials whose work it is supposed to supervise. So they supervise themselves. But who are these officials? Except for the specialists, they are, as we have seen, people without education or specialties, who in practical terms can, solely by the chairman's will, be removed from their brigade leaderships to become simple collective farmers the very next day. Incidentally that means a one-half to two-thirds reduction in earnings. I have heard nothing unfavorable about G. A. Smirnov—he is a good man, efficient and capable, but you cannot get away from the objective arguments: He is in charge of both the farm and the community.

And when he says jokingly, "Yes, we remember about education when a correspondent comes here," his joke expresses the profound conflict of his position. For who is speaking when he says that? The leader of the village community or the organizer of production? As leader, he must be interested in the maximum intelligence level of the community. But as organizer of a specific production operation at its present technological and organizational level, sometimes—as in the case of animal husbandry, for example—how educated the workers are matters to him not at all. As leader, he should have become alarmed at learning, say, from my research on the village store's bookkeeping, that, while the consumption of printed matter has remained the same in the village for the last five years, the consumption of alcoholic beverages has more than doubled. As organizer, he merely shrugged his shoulders.

The duality of the chairman's functions arose historically from the harsh necessity to subordinate the entire life of rural society at a certain stage in its development to the interests of production. But should a temporary need be turned into a permanent virtue? Especially when, in some places today, it is already hindering further democratization of rural society and the involvement in management of the two decisive social forces in the village, young people and the intelligentsia?

This was the comment of one reader, whose letter appeared in Literaturnaya gazeta *on February 7, 1968:*

Zmiyev, Kharkov Province—I read Yanov's article about what they have thought up in Kostroma: paying young people at higher rates.

The very fact that a fellow or girl fresh out of school will be paid more than an experienced milkmaid deals a hard moral blow to the milkmaid, who will never understand the expediency of such "benefits." In my opinion, to do this is to take the line of least resistance, and, what's more, it violates our basic principle of payment according to labor. I do not believe this experiment will succeed.

In my opinion, this is what should be done: Double and

"Sitting pretty" (*Krokodil*, No. 3, 1969)

triple the rate of mechanization of agricultural production, above all animal husbandry. It is necessary, moreover, to reorganize in radical fashion the cultural cast of the countryside and rural living conditions. And, finally, it is essential to resolve, and without delay, the question of roads, without which nothing at all can be done in the countryside.—L. Veselovsky, economist.

> *A quite different view of the problems of the collective farm is presented in the following excerpt by Andrei Amalrik, who, in the mid-1960's, when he was in his twenties, spent time working on a farm as punishment for his unorthodox views on other subjects. The selection is from his book* Involuntary Journey to Siberia, *translated by Manya Harari and Max Hayward, (New York: Harcourt Brace Jovanovich, A Helen and Kurt Wolff Book, 1970). It has been published in the West but not in the Soviet Union.*

It seems to me that overhasty collectivization and the forced pace of industrial development at the expense of agriculture were a great mistake for which the country has paid dearly in both political and economic terms. The only possible way to put this right is to give agriculture large transfusions of capital.

I am not a specialist in agriculture and have read virtually nothing on economics, but during the time I worked on the *kolkhoz* [collective farm] I made a number of observations that I should like to summarize here. The prime condition for a sensible use of any new capital investment, and for the efficient running of agriculture in particular, seems to me to be the granting of much greater independence to the *kolkhozy*. It is essential to give up not only the detailed supervision of their work but the whole system of planning it from above. Each *kolkhoz* should be allowed to make its own plan, which it would submit to the state, not for approval but simply for information, to enable the authorities to form an over-all picture. The state could continue to regulate agricultural production through its fixing of wholesale prices (a sensible policy in regard to these is also, incidentally, a matter of urgent importance). In my view the state should put pressure on the *kolkhozy* not to step up production in quantitative terms, but to raise the quality of their output. I further believe that the independence of the *kolkhozy* can be achieved only through the independence of its individual members. If the *kolkhoz* chairman is to be made independent of the district authorities (to whom at the moment he is completely subordinated), then he should be appointed by the *kolkhozniki* themselves in real elections and should be truly accountable to them. The need is not to "further develop *kolkhoz* democracy," to use the empty newspaper phrase, but to create, virtually from scratch, genuinely democratic attitudes in the *kolkhozy*. Without this it will be impossible to make the *kolkhozniki* feel that the development of agriculture depends primarily on their own individual efforts. They will achieve more only if they have a feeling of self-respect and personal responsibility for their jobs.

CULTURAL FACILITIES IN

WESTERN SIBERIA

Frankly, what follows is the kind of material that scares readers away. It is a collection of data about clubs and libraries and recreational facilities in the villages of two districts in Western Siberia. Yet to get a real sense of life in the deep countryside, it is worth going through these figures—from the sheer repetition and accumulation of them, you begin to feel what the possibilities actually are: where people can go in their spare time and what they can do. Bear in mind that when a village library or a movie is, let us say, ten kilometers away, this does not mean hopping in your own car and driving there on a paved road in a matter of fifteen minutes. The few cars out in the countryside are for Party and government business, and the transportation is overwhelmingly by truck and bus.

The selection is taken from the book Sotsialnye problemy trudovykh resursov sela (Social Problems of the Labor Resources of the Village), *edited by T. I. Zaslavskaya (Novosibirsk, 1968).*

The following data give an idea of the level of cultural facilities. In both regions, ninety-three out of one hundred twenty-three settlements, or 75 per cent, have a club, a house of culture, and a reading room. All of the small villages with fewer than 100 inhabitants are lacking these facilities, and so are one-third of the medium-sized villages (with 100–300 inhabitants) in the remote parts of Sedelnikovo District. Of thirty-two villages that make use of clubs in other places, nine are up to four kilometers away, fourteen are five to nine kilometers away, and seven are at least ten kilometers away from the clubs they use.

Only forty-two villages have libraries: twenty in Okoneshnikovo District and twenty-two in Sedelnikovo District. The people in the remote parts of Sedelnikovo District are the best off; they have libraries not only in all of the big villages (with populations of more than 500) but also in two villages with populations of from 101 to 200 people, in ten with populations of 201–300, and in seven with populations of 301–500 people. In Okoneshnikovo District, only twenty out of thirty villages with populations of more than 300 have libraries. Only six villages in Okoneshnikovo District and only twelve in Sedelnikovo District have access to libraries in neighboring villages that are less than four kilometers away. Of the other fifty-eight villages in the two districts together, thirty-eight use libraries at a distance of five to nine kilometers and twenty use libraries that are ten or more kilometers away.

In the bulletins that every club puts out describing its work, there was information about the cultural activities that had taken place in the first six months of 1965. There were films, amateur talent evenings, dances, lectures, and, only once in a great while, plays. The larger the village, the more movies, evening programs, and lectures there were. In the large villages movies are shown three or four times a week, and in the district centers there are as many as three or four showings a day. There are also eight villages that have not seen a movie for six months and six where a movie is shown only once a month. Of course, things are worse in the remote parts of the district, especially in the small and medium-sized villages. In the summer, the young people of those villages can see a movie in the neighboring village, but even this is not always accessible. The inhabitants of seven villages have to go five to nine kilometers, and those of four villages have to go more than ten kilometers to see a movie.

Besides movies, the most widespread cultural recreation in the two districts are amateur talent shows. In the first half of 1965, such shows took place in practically all the big villages and in the majority of the medium-sized villages. In fifty-one settlements there were at least three such talent shows during that period, in twenty-five villages there were two, and in eleven there was one show. In thirty-six places there was not even one. Only the twenty-five largest villages put on plays.

About one-half of all the medium-sized and large villages have dances one or two evenings a week. In the small villages there are none. In most of the settlements there are lectures every month. However, in twelve villages (including two with populations of 300–500) there was not a single lecture in six months.

It remains to be added that forty out of the one hundred twenty-three settlements did not have radio broadcast relay centers, and in seventeen villages there was not a single radio. It is gratifying that there are television sets in forty out of fifty-four villages in the more accessible parts of Okoneshnikovo District. In the remote parts, evidently because of the great distances involved, there is no television. It should be noted that ten small villages in that district had no electricity. To sum up, the possibilities for entertainment and cultural recreation are not so great in the big villages, and they are very limited in the medium-sized villages, while in the small villages they are practically nonexistent.

In conditions where most of the cultural facilities and everyday services are concentrated in the district centers or in just a few villages, it is of decisive importance to have regularly functioning means of transportation within the district. A bus runs through forty out of fifty-four settlements in Okoneshnikovo District, two villages are one to four kilometers from the nearest bus stop, and ten villages are more than five kilometers away from a regular bus route. In Sedelnikovo District, only eleven out of sixty-nine settlements are located on a bus route, and ten are less than five kilometers from a bus stop. The inhabitants of the remaining forty-eight villages have to go more than five kilometers to get to a bus, and for the inhabitants of twenty-eight villages the distance is up to ten kilometers and more. The people in villages far from the bus routes can only hope for a lift from a vehicle that happens to be passing through.

Leaving Dawn Collective Farm and "burning his bridges behind him" (*Krokodil*, No. 32, 1969)

ZINA'S CLUB

"Not enough culture" is a frequent reply that comes high on the list of reasons young people give for leaving the farms. Many villages do have cultural clubs, and it is interesting to see what goes on in them, what people think of them, and how attitudes are changing as the village begins to acquire some of the material conveniences and recreational tastes of the city. This. article tells how a visiting Soviet journalist from the city sees the problems of a woman who has the difficult and lonely job of creating culture almost from scratch in the club of a good-sized village. The article appeared in the magazine Selskaya molodezh *(Village Youth), No. 5, 1969.*

"The village is a fine one and the people are interesting. In a word, this is the Volgograd region—earth that is figuratively saturated with the rains and thunderstorms of history. Everything here evokes associations. Wherever you turn there is stimulus for educational and cultural work.

"And the landscape? Well, this place seems to have been specially conceived for a university of aesthetics. The Don River and the steppe.

"Although your state farm is just an average one in the district, it has a chance of becoming one of the leading farms. And a large part of its success, Zina, depends on you. There are 600 inhabitants in Peskovatka—that is a tremendous force —and your club has hundreds of ways of exerting a good influence on production.

"I envy you, Zina—I really do! The people here love you; they understand and value you. And everything you do turns out well. It's not for nothing that your club holds first place in the district."

That is the "monologue" I had prepared for my first meeting with Zina. By the second meeting I was already thinking differently.

"Oh, how hard it is for you. And there is no one to whom you can take your grievances. You are the whole club. The comforter and the receiving center for all the complaints about boredom.

"And the people are always the same ones. Naturally. A village club is not a touring troupe, continually on the road and always appearing before a different audience. From its windows there is just one view that never changes—Peskovatka.

"So you come to the club and there is no one inside. It's cold and empty. The village is close by and at the same time terribly far away. People are waiting to see what you will come up with. Maybe they're not even waiting—most likely they're not. They haven't time for that; they have their own concerns and duties. All right, so what are we going to do? Light the stove? Paint some posters? Or get on the telephone and work on the village Soviet to find a new movie projectionist for the district? The last one was drafted into the army this week."

I put myself mentally in Zina's place. But she, meanwhile, talks about the club confidently and energetically, and even in her thoughts there is no sign of feeling blue or giving in.

"We are tired of presentations built around a single topic. It's true, we draw almost everyone in that way, but you can sense that something isn't right. And the same goes for the

'Spoken Journal' evenings. The audience is one part and the
stage is another—two halves—and between them is a boundary of apathy, disguised as deference to the importance of the
subject under discussion.

"On the whole, the 'Ogonyok' parties have been a life-
saver. On those evenings there isn't that boundary—everyone
is onstage, because everyone who comes is a participant. We
invite those people to whom the evening is dedicated, and we
pay attention to each one of them—nobody is left out. The
last 'Ogonyok' party we had was dedicated to young people.
They all sat at tables and helped themselves to lemonade,
coffee, and champagne—whatever they wanted. The veteran
Komsomol [Young Communist League] members and the
young ones all sat together. There was a mixture of songs and
poetry, stories by the Komsomol members of the 1920's and
speeches by those of the 1960's. I was the mistress of cere-
monies; I had prepared my remarks ahead of time—I don't
feel I'm articulate enough to speak off the top of my head.

"Then there was dancing. The old Komsomol members
danced too, whereas on other evenings, organized differently,
they wouldn't have danced—they wouldn't have let themselves go like that. It didn't matter if you were twenty years
old or fifty—everybody took part, and they all knew one another, and it was their evening. They say that if you seat people at tables and give them wine, they end up getting rowdy.
But that didn't happen to us."

Zina has her own peculiar way of speaking. As if perceiv-
ing an opponent inside herself, she fixes her gray-blue eyes on
one spot and argues.

While she talks, this is most likely what she is thinking: "I
hope he understands and isn't just going to shower more
praise on us. Still, there's no need for us to humble ourselves
—we're no worse than the others. Of course, it's true that we
didn't get first place for nothing, but that was more like an
advance, a show of confidence in us. We don't even have any

musical instruments—the choir and the soloists sing without accompaniment. If you counted up all our shortcomings, you could demolish us. If he's come to criticize, to give us a good dressing down, well, that too is unfair.

"All right then, let him write—what do we care? We'll still be as we are now—with no accordionist, with a broken radio. As for getting a television set, I don't even think about that. And what do we need one for anyway? We have movies. But I wish they'd fix the ceiling; it's coming down."

Zina grumbles to herself; she's not very contented with herself, or with her work and her life.

But her club is cosy and clean, and not the kind of clean that looks as if it had been cleaned for the first time yesterday.

There is nothing superfluous hanging on the walls. What is there is arranged in a restrained and cultivated way. The honor roll. "The Soldiers Returning in 1945"—photographs of demobilized village men coming home after the Great Patriotic War. "They Serve the Homeland with Merit"—snapshots of Peskovatka men who are doing their military service now. And there is a photo display dedicated to Vladimir Ilyich [Lenin].

I recall a palace of culture I saw in Volgograd; it has a staff of fifty-four people. Here, Zina is alone.

An amateur talent show—now, that is the hardest thing of all to organize. People would be glad enough to do it in working hours, but don't expect them to give up a summer evening when they've just come in from the fields—everybody has his own preoccupations. The movie is over at midnight or, if there's a documentary film with it, 1:00 a.m. Only then can you rehearse for the talent show, and the rehearsing sometimes goes on until three in the morning. And what about all the persuasion you have to exert on people? And the strain of the whole thing?

There was a time when amateur talent shows were perhaps a novelty. But now people are even a little ashamed to take part in them. Besides, they have television sets and radios in their homes. The old timers say that people used to walk as far as fifteen kilometers to any organized activity. Now they won't go more than a step except by truck or car.

In those days people were more active. Now they are more literate and discriminating and—passive?

Powers? What powers does the head of a village club have? Nobody knows. According to the existing popular view about the club, he doesn't need to have any powers. No one has worked out the sociological situation of the village club; no one has coordinated all of its various aspects—economic, ju-dicial, and administrative.

Officially, it is subordinate to the district cultural section [of the Party] and to the village Soviet. But it cannot expect to get along without, in addition, keeping on the good side of the state farm director. And each of those patrons has its own idea of the club, its own objectives, and its own claims upon it. The village Soviet, for example, asks the club every year for a census of the population and of people's livestock and land-holdings.

The cultural section wants a plan and a report, listing lec-tures, visual propaganda, amateur talent shows, "Spoken Journal" evenings, and so forth.

"Give us a concert!" says the head office of the farm.

"Help raise production!" says the cultural section.

"Entertainment!" say the people of the village.

There are many pensioners now in Peskovatka, and you have to work with them, too. What does that mean? With each one, a special relationship, your own relationship. Old people are very cautious about accepting new things. Fash-ions, for example. At first they just sneered at the straight shift dresses; now they themselves wear them. The same holds true with respect to music and dancing. At first they said, "In the old days people really knew how to dance. But this is not dancing." Then they grew accustomed to it, and it was as if they had forgotten their initial hostility.

The young people have their own customs and traditions. On holidays they gather in groups in different people's homes. Each has his circle of friends, which has developed over the years. Zina knows them all, she's at home everywhere, and little by little she tries gently to bring all these "home" clubs more often into one general group, without destroying any of the inner ties.

Personal relations—that's a special subject, of course. Liusia was left alone with her child and her ruined hopes. It seems that she didn't lament over Vasili for very long. He stopped loving her, so what could she do? It was just tough luck.

Then Viktor came to the village temporarily to do some work. He and Liusia developed a close relationship. Before their wedding, Viktor left the village to get his identification papers to register the marriage. Just then, Vasili turned up in the village, either by accident or because he had heard that Viktor was away. He went up to Liusia at a dance and from then on never left her. Again, their heads were spinning and their feelings revived, and they went back to living together.

But then Viktor returned. It was hard for Liusia. How can one give advice at such a time? Yet advice was needed. "Stay with the father of your child," Zina said.

So what will happen to the village club? Will it turn into a cafe? A movie house or a theater? When we grow more rich, Peskovatka will have all those things. And a club too. But what will it be like? Who will head it, and what kind of abilities will he have? Will he be just a routine organizer of many activities?

I remember what started me off on all this, the thoughts I had about Zina. She does not set these monologues apart and counterpose one to the other. For her they are all part of the same whole—the consciousness of joy and misfortune, of holidays and gray days, of doubts and responsibility.

POLITICAL EDUCATION

ON A FARM

Besides providing recreation, the village club holds meetings to inform the peasants about political developments and to explain Party policies to them. Andrei Amalrik conveys the flavor of such meetings on the collective farm where he worked near Tomsk, in Siberia. The excerpt is, again, from Involuntary Journey to Siberia.

Just before the first of May the *kolkhozniki* were given a lecture on the international and domestic situation by a lecturer sent out by the district Party committee. Up to then most of the propaganda work in the village had been conducted by Vera, the manager of the recreation room, who from time to time somewhat incoherently read from newspaper articles, which she barely understood herself, and then explained to us—an article on Sinyavsky and Daniel [writers who were convicted of "slander against the state" in 1965], for example, she reduced to the simple proposition that they were American spies. She also read off to us day after day the infinitely long-winded statement issued at the end of the Twenty-third Congress of the CPSU [Communist Party of the Soviet Union]. Hardly anyone listened, however, since they were too busy with their work; if they did listen, it made no sense, because they didn't even know what CPSU meant.

One schoolboy asked her what it meant, but she wasn't able to tell him. Only Filimon, the mechanic in charge of the milking machinery, who had once attended a course in the city, was able to say what it was.

The lecture was given in the school. The lecturer, who had a round, good-humored face and looked like a well-read peasant, began by saying he had been at a meeting in Tomsk at which he and other lecturers had been briefed by Obrikov, a representative of the Central Committee of the CPSU, and that he would now be giving us the gist of what he had been told there. The main point of his talk was that not only abroad, but even inside the country, there were people who did not believe that the domestic situation was good, but thought some things were wrong. Since it was impossible to make such people change their minds, Party lecturers had now been instructed to admit that there were indeed shortcomings in the country. "In particular, comrades," he said, "as you well know yourselves, our agriculture is in a very bad way." He explained this, with an air of great shrewdness, by saying that our country was a very large one with too much variety in climatic conditions. By this he evidently meant to imply that, though conditions vary all over the country, the authorities expected everybody to obey the same instructions. He also said that Soviet tractors were too heavy and cumbersome. After this he spoke only about our strong points, the chief of which was the military might of our country. He said that on this score—unlike agriculture—we had no reason for anxiety at all. He condemned the Americans for the war in Vietnam, attacked West Germany, and praised France. About China he said: "They live even worse than we do." Since many people in the village had heard Chinese broadcasts, they asked him a few questions: Who is helping Vietnam most, we or the Chinese, and is it possible that we might become friends with China again? He said the Chinese were helping Vietnam only in words, and that it was quite possible that we would be friendly with them again after the death of Mao Tse-tung. He ended his lecture on a quite unexpected note by saying we should not worry about the fate of Khrushchev, who was living at liberty in Moscow and was not complaining about his life.

A month later we got another lecture, this time in the recreation room, and after it there was a concert. On this occasion the lecturer was a rather pretty girl who, constantly wringing her thin hands, spoke in a hushed voice, mostly about the war in Vietnam. When she invited questions, Leva, who had fought in the Korean War, drunkenly got to his feet and said he was very interested to hear about events in Vietnam, because he had once been in Korea. "When were you there?" asked the girl sweetly. Delighted to be taken notice of, Leva replied: "I was there in the days when we used to sing that song 'Stalin and Mao Are Listening to Us.'" He then tried to start singing it but was quickly made to sit down. The concert was given by a group from one of the Tomsk factories. First a small chorus sang a song about comradeship among soldiers and then one about rockets standing at the ready. Next somebody sang a song about how we should not forget the last war and should be prepared for the next. Finally someone recited a poem on the same general theme.

After the first lecture in the school, we had a meeting to decide the question of who would graze the cattle during the coming summer months.

LETTER FROM A GRANDMOTHER

A grandmother who also happens to be the chairman of a collective farm expressed her view about changes that have taken place in the village in her lifetime. Having gone through very hard times before her farm reached a level of at least some prosperity, she now finds much to puzzle about in the attitude of today's young people. Her letter was published in Komsomolskaya pravda (Young Communist League Truth) *on April 21, 1968.*

I wanted to write about our weddings, but this is turning out to be about something quite different. Well, I'll just write what comes.

I wanted to write about the weddings because here in Samet we have fine ones, cheerful ones, yes, and lots of them. On those days virtually the whole village gathers in the Palace of Culture, and people even come from other villages. The chairman of the village Soviet registers the young couple's marriage, and I give them gold rings and present the gifts. Each time, I get emotional. It seems to me one never gets used to weddings. On a wedding day you can see in the faces of the elderly women delight and radiant maternal joy and a secret womanly sadness. Of course there are always shouts of "bitter" [which calls for the bride and groom to kiss and make things sweet again], and parting words that make the bride blush: "We wish you children, lots of them."

How long we sometimes have to wait for the children! I write this not only as a collective farm chairman who is already laughed at in the district. "Well, Praskovya, you've gone and built a nursery, and who will go to your nursery?" I am troubled by this cautiousness of our young couples; what it comes from, I don't know. From thinking, perhaps? Maybe from not thinking? Because, what kind of a family is it that has no children's voices? And for a woman, what kind of happiness can there be without children? In earlier days in the village the smallest family had five people. My great-grandmother on my father's side, Darya Ivanovna Gavricheva, had eighteen children.

Nowadays, in these new times, some of the young wives want no part of woman's eternal bustling about with babies—hard work, of course, but giving so much joy and so much that is human and cannot be provided by anything else. They say, "For the time being we'll live for ourselves, and then we'll see." I simply can't understand where such a philosophy comes from. Here we have more or less grown wealthy, the bridegroom takes his bride with more than just the one dress to her name, and, if you look into a newlyweds' house, you will see a television set, a washing machine, and a set of matching furniture, too. Why is it, one asks, that our young couples in the village now have a different view about family life? Was it for this that the farm and we grew richer, that we trod the hard road together for so many years, in order now not to rejoice in an abundant collective farm tribe?

The first "Fordson" [tractor], for example, came to our Samet as far back as 1929. Then electricity appeared. We saved kopeks so we could buy pedigreed cattle, we saved up to build a school, and from morning till evening we toiled away at the harvest. My oldest daughter, Lidushka, was born while I was out mowing hay. I simply laid her in a haystack—then I forgot which one, and it's a good thing Lidushka started to cry. And now our collective farm women have lived to see paid maternity leaves (the payments are sizable, about 300 rubles), nurseries, and an excellent school.

Not long ago I went to visit our kindergarten. The children are well fed and well cared for. They surrounded me and made a hubbub. "Aunt Panya, we will give you a concert." Oh, if only there were three times, four times as many children! I hear that in the cities there's not enough space in the kindergartens, but we have so much! Just recently we opened a new eight-year school. And what do you know? There was almost no one to enter the first grade.

Here is the question that troubles me: To whom will we, the older collective farm generation, pass on the wealth we have accumulated? Today I am writing so that we can all think about this together.—Praskovya Malinina, Chairman, October Twelfth Collective Farm, Kostroma Province.

PART TWO

Conversations with and About Young People in the City

One day in Moscow in the summer of 1969 I ran into three girls and a boy who were eager to practice their English with a visiting American. We went into the park nearby and sat on a bench and talked. As you will see from our conversation, their English was quite good—I have only tidied up a few grammatical rough spots. Some words about the youngsters themselves: They are sixteen years old and entering their last year of high school, which in Russia is the tenth grade; they go to one of Moscow's many "special" schools, where a foreign language is introduced earlier and taught more thoroughly than in the regular schools; they are privileged youngsters with fathers in the high establishment, and their *views reflect this fact. When we started talking, they were clearly conscious of a certain sense of responsibility for the picture I was getting of the Soviet Union. But their own natural enthusiasms and views were also there.*

A Moscow park

FOUR HIGH SCHOOL STUDENTS

TRY OUT THEIR ENGLISH

Question: What would you say are the goals of the young people you know? Do they want a more comfortable life? Are they idealistic?

NATASHA: I suppose the thing we most want is knowledge, because now we are grown up, and we understand that nothing can be done without knowledge.

LENA: The passion for truth is very strong. In our country we can't do without it, even in our relations with our parents.

TANYA: To my mind the only thing for us to do is get as much knowledge as possible. I am for the romantic outlook when we have free time. I don't think our youth just wants to get a car and a television set, because this is not enough of a program for us. It is not the aim of life. They want these things of course, but they are not living only for them.

LENA: On the whole, our country is very romantic, with a little bit of realism. A lot of students have gone to Siberia and the Far East to work there, and they want cars and television sets, but they work for their own pleasure and satisfaction too. If I enter the university, I shall go to Siberia with all the students. It is their custom to help the workers during summer vacations, and I suppose it is very interesting out there, and I would like to go.

Question: Would you say that young people are becoming more independent in their thinking?

LENA: Perhaps it is true, because now there are no heroes whom we can personally admire, and we have to combine all the heroes and take what we need from each one of them. And the characteristic features of this combination are what will suit us and not any one single person. In this way youth is independent—taking only some features and not the whole person.

Question: What characteristics do you admire most?

LENA: I think it is courage—mostly courage.

TANYA: I would also say courage, and yes, of course, will power. And a strong love for truth—this goes without saying.

NATASHA: I would choose will power.

Question: You spoke of your relations with your parents. What are the difficulties?

LENA: On the whole, our mothers and fathers understand us. The problems are mini skirts and our interest in popular dances and long hair and in every modern current that comes over us. Only here is there a problem. In school, it is forbidden to wear very mini skirts, but the girls try.

Question: Are there any changes you would like to see in the school? Any reforms that you think are needed?

LENA: I think our system of education is all right now, and the only thing that must be changed is that more writers should be included in the reading program and some who are already there should be taken out. For example, I would like to see Harper Lee's *To Kill a Mockingbird* included.

NATASHA: I suppose the problem of the curriculum is not settled yet and is still open to discussion. It is very difficult to settle whether we must have more mathematics or more literature, more languages or more physics and chemistry. I think the only thing we can do is to let the pupil study those subjects in which he is interested. We already have specialized schools for mathematics and foreign languages. Maybe we'll soon have more specialized classes and studies for other subjects in which we are interested. But it is a question of time—we don't have enough for all we want to learn.

Question: How do you spend your free time?

NATASHA: At school we very often have evening parties. Because a lot of our day goes into reading and writing, when we have free time we try to spend it away from home, out of the apartment. We try to go for a walk and be more active. We are fond of skiing and skating in winter. We go to the countryside with our whole class and spend our free time there. We like outdoor sports.

Question: Do you listen to jazz and rock? Are there any good jazz ensembles here?

SERGEI: Yes, there are many groups in high schools and in the institutes. I like the Beatles and the Rolling Stones and a lot of others, and in Moscow you can find the same types of groups as the Beatles—a lot of them, in fact, because this kind of music is very popular in our country.

LENA: Nowadays the most popular singers are Edith Piaf and Charles Aznavour, and Salvatore Adamo is popular, too. Next year it may be different.

Question: What are your relations with the boys like at this stage? Do young people tend to get married early?

TANYA: We meet often at the evening parties. We like to go together to the theater or perhaps on a trip. But it's always in groups, sometimes large groups and even whole classes. There is a great friendship among all of us, because we have studied together in the same school from the first grade to the tenth grade.

LENA: Our law forbids marriage until the age of eighteen. There are some cases of people getting married before that time, but they are not usual. I am speaking about our part of the country, because in Central Asia many girls marry at a younger age. In our ninth grade class the relations between boys and girls are very strange—they do everything in groups—but in other grades, for example in the tenth, there are pairs and they prefer to walk and to meet by themselves, in pairs.

TANYA: In the universities there are cases of marriage and children being born, but it is very difficult for wives and mothers to study if they have little children, and that's why they try to avoid this.

NATASHA: Now we are still studying in high school and I guess this is why we don't know these problems in detail, because we haven't come in touch with them yet.

Question: Is there any interest among young people in old Russian culture?

LENA: I think that our teacher of history gave us a great love for Russian culture, for our ancient churches and old buildings, because she is fond of them and thanks to her we love them too.

NATASHA: We are grateful to her because she taught us to understand the beauty of Russian architecture and ancient Russian art, and now we like it very much. And when we have free time we try to go to some suburbs of Moscow to see the monuments of architecture.

SERGEI: And we like our Central Asia very much. It has very beautiful and unusual architecture.

Question: How do you feel about Stalin? What is your estimate of him?

LENA: You see, Stalin did a lot for our country, and gave his help during the war and after the war, but he made a lot of mistakes during his life. He decided everything alone, and that's why there were many mistakes in his orders to people. Now these mistakes have been discovered and our government is trying to escape them, and that is why Stalin is not so popular and not so admired as he was fifteen or twenty years ago.

SERGEI: Stalin was the great leader of our country and he did much for it, but he made mistakes. All the power in our country belonged to the Supreme Soviet [the Soviet Union's parliament], and in spite of this Stalin did everything himself, and that was the trouble.

NATASHA: History knows that when power is concentrated in the hands of one man, it is difficult for him to rule honestly. But I suppose that now this question is no longer the burning one of our days, and the problem is settled.

TANYA: Yes, it never occurred to me to discuss this problem, and I am not interested in it.

Question: What do people think about China these days?

LENA: I think that the incidents on Damansky Island [the fighting between Soviet and Chinese troops on the border in March, 1969] prove that the policy of the Chinese Government is wrong, our help wasn't worthwhile, and they are not grateful and don't remember it. And I think Mao will not lead the Chinese people for long. Then, perhaps, the Communist Party of China will gather their people all over China, gather their forces, and do something better with them.

Question: Will bad relations with China lead to better ones with the United States, do you think?

LENA: I don't know what to say, really, because the problem of China and the problem of the West are so difficult for us and also for our government that I cannot guess anything.

SERGEI: I think our country must have better relations with the United States. Trade between our countries must be increased, and we must be closer.

Question: Is the fear of a large war very much on people's minds?

NATASHA: You see, when we are asked what is the most terrifying fact in our lives, I suppose most of us would say that it is war, because in our minds it is the most horrible thing in the world.

TANYA: Our people know what war means, we lived through all this.

LENA: I think that war has touched every family in the Soviet Union. Our grandfathers and grandmothers and even our fathers and mothers lived through the war, and we see what it cost them. Many of them returned wounded, and now, in the streets, we can see disabled men, and they are suffering even in days of peace. That's why in our everyday life we meet with war.

NATASHA: We haven't lived through the war, but with our own eyes we see the results of it, and that is why the struggle for peace is the everyday and most burning question of our times.

Question: What is your system of military service?

SERGEI: If we study in an institute or at the university, we won't have to go into the military service. But if we don't continue our full-time studies, we will have to go into the service. Even in the institutes and at the university, there is also a department of the military where we must learn subjects having to do with war. So I think that one way or another we must serve in our army.

Question: Why was it that so few people here spoke out against your invasion of Czechoslovakia [in August, 1968]?

NATASHA: We suppose that socialism was in danger there. We agree with the policy of our government, but, you see, we do not know enough to speak in details—we are not competent to speak about it.

Question: Do you read about what goes on in the West? About our students and what they are thinking?

NATASHA: Some time ago I read your book *Up the Down Staircase* by Bel Kaufman. I don't know, but to my mind it depicts very well the system of education in your country and the life of students. I liked it very much, and now I hope to see the film. So I suppose that this book gave me very much knowledge about life there.

Question: Do you think that you have any feelings and attitudes in common with the students in the West?

SERGEI: I think we are very much like the students of the United States and England. We have the same aspirations: We don't want war, we like to study, we want to have much knowledge, and we have the same troubles.

SPEAKING FREELY—

MASHA, YURI, AND ZOYA

I talked with several other young people in Moscow, separately and in private surroundings, where they felt secure enough to express their thoughts and feelings on a wide range of subjects. They spoke in Russian, and I have tried to preserve in translation the informal and free-flowing quality of their conversation.

Masha is seventeen years old and has just graduated from high school. She is interested in literature and has done some writing herself, which only her family and friends have read. They encourage her to go on in this field and she plans to, but first she wants to get away from studying and have a job for a year or so. "That way," she says, "I'll have time to collect myself and be more confident about what I want to do with my life."

In our school the teachers are on the whole fairly decent. They are curious about us and always seem to know what's going on—who's in love with whom—but they don't interfere too much. We behave quite independently toward them. In English class the teacher would say, "Let's translate a passage," and we would answer, "No, we're not prepared today." In literature class, we were asked to write about the difference between the societies of *chinovniki* [petty bureau-crats] before the Revolution in *The Inspector General* and *Dead Souls*, two works by [the nineteenth-century author] Gogol. One girl announced that she would not write on that theme, because there was no difference whatsoever. Another time, a new literature teacher came to the ninth grade in the middle of the school year and said to us, "I want to get acquainted with you quickly because there is not much time left, so will each of you please write me an essay telling me all about yourself." Everyone did, except for one girl who wrote on a literary theme instead, and when the teacher asked her why, the girl said, "You can only tell a really good friend all about yourself, and I hardly even know you." The point is that we feel stronger than our teachers, and better educated. They belong to a different generation, and they don't quite know how to manage us. We want to be wild and impetuous and to seize the whole of life at once. But we understand that our teachers are well entrenched and that it is useless to get into serious conflict with them—it doesn't lead anywhere, at least not to any improvements—so we pretty much take things as they are and try to go our own way outside of school.

The thirteen-, fourteen-, and fifteen-year-olds here love the detective stories of Simenon and Conan Doyle and, later on, Agatha Christie. At sixteen and seventeen, many of us turn to the classics. I love Pushkin and Lermontov—the girls, especially, find the Pushkin period very romantic. And Tolstoy and Dostoyevsky—I love the contrast between them. We often talk about these Russian writers of the nineteenth century among ourselves and argue over their works. We find a lot of resonance in Tolstoy's novel *War and Peace*, something there for everyone to think about. I love Chekhov and Alexei Tolstoy, and Bulgakov—his *Master and Margarita*—but I don't much like the Soviet writers of our time, except for some of the poets—Voznesensky, Yevtushenko, Akhmadul-lina, and, of course, Pasternak. Our teacher introduced us to

Solzhenitsyn, told us he is a very good writer, and urged us to read him. Among Western writers, Remarque is still fairly well liked, and the classics of O. Henry, de Maupassant, and Molière. Some people read Scott Fitzgerald. Salinger, the American novelist, is really popular, especially with the boys—they see themselves in his teenage hero, Holden Caulfield.

We read *Komsomolskaya pravda* [*Young Communist League Truth*, the newspaper of the Young Communist League] a lot, and *Literaturnaya gazeta* [*Literary Gazette*], and sometimes *Smena* [*Generation*, a Young Communist League monthly]. I used to read *Yunost* [*Youth*], but now it has fallen behind and is often boring. I don't read *Pravda* and *Izvestia* (the leading Party and government newspapers). We listen to the Voice of America and to our Soviet radio; we're quite sensitive and can sense what is being concealed. The parents of my friends are in touch with politics, and we learn from them something about what is going on in the world. We hear things about the students abroad, but at our level we do not feel we are plugged into any international youth movement.

We argued a lot about Czechoslovakia among ourselves, and people had different views about our soldiers' going in there, but we did not express our views in class or to our teachers. My grandfather is an old revolutionary who believes everything he reads and hears. My generation may be less experienced in politics and revolution than his, but I think our views are closer to the truth of life than those of his generation.

A few years ago, some tenth graders in our school formed a secret group and started to work out a platform of their social and political views. In general, what they wanted was more freedom. They sent a letter to the Central Committee protesting against the trials of the writers, and a second letter in support of a partial rehabilitation of Stalin. They condemned the terror of the 1930's and 1940's but said that in spite of his crimes Stalin was an illustrious personality who did a lot for the country and should be honored for his contribution. I know it seems strange that the same people should write those two letters. The point is that it is not so much the substance as the idea of protest, the idea of being independent. I think it is a sign of distrust of what is going on around us. At any rate, the people in that group were not very serious types and went about their work rather stupidly, and they were soon found out and given a formal reprimand. And two young teachers who sympathized with them were expelled from the school.

The "Metelitsa" cafe opened in the late 1960's. Here young Moscovites eat ice cream and drink wine, beer, or "koktaili."

What do we do in our free time and to amuse ourselves? Well, we have dances at school four or five times a year. In between, we get together in somebody's apartment and there is always one among us who plays the guitar and sings. We go to a favorite cafe—this past year it has been the Metelitsa —and we dance there, eat ice cream and oranges, and drink *koktaili*, which are mostly made of wine, fruit juice, and ice and served in a tall glass for about seventy-five kopeks [eighty-three cents]. There used to be a jazz ensemble there and lots of inventive dancing, but the Komsomol activists thought things were getting out of control—they couldn't keep order. So they dismissed the band, and now there are only phonograph records to dance to. My favorite singers are Salvatore Adamo and Enrico Macias—they are both French, and their songs are very lyrical, about how they love the sun and love life. Our most popular dance these days is the shake in slow rhythm. We love gentle movements; the fast ones are less fashionable than they used to be. In Moscow, you hardly ever see two girls dancing with one another any more—it's considered bad form now. There are other good cafes in town, some of them where you just talk and listen to music, but the Metelitsa has been popular this year because it is new, and the people who gather there are mostly young.

We love to travel about the country, two or three friends together, going to Leningrad, the Baltic coast, the Black Sea and the Crimea. In ninth grade we took a group tour with our teacher to the old Russian cities of Rostov and Suzdal. We love to see the old churches in those places. We like to go out to the countryside, walk in the woods, swim, and just be at the dacha [country house]. Summer and autumn are my favorite times of the year. New Year's Eve is a great time too; we always gather somewhere and have a festive party. We love to gaze into a bowl of water or a mirror and tell each other's fortunes. We love the evening of May Day, when there are fireworks and floodlights, and cars are banned from the main streets so that people can walk and dance under the lights.

You ask about our relationships with the boys. This is the main thing on everybody's mind, I think. Everyone is in love and suffering over somebody. We do a lot of kissing, but there is no sleeping together among my friends. Maybe the boys do with girls outside our school, but not with us—we don't feel ready for this yet and I know nineteen- and twenty-year-old girls who still haven't slept with a boy. They are waiting for some decent fellow who is not going to attack them on the next street corner. My school is a privileged one; most of us come from families of the intelligentsia, so the boys behave pretty well. Except when they drink, and there is quite a lot of drinking.

The girls say that they want to have children but do not want to get married. At this stage they don't think they will ever find an ideal man, and they want to be independent. Many of the boys in my class are going into math or physics. Everyone wants to go abroad for a visit, and some think about this so much that they try to get into the Institute of International Affairs with the idea of becoming a diplomat. The girls tend to prefer the humanities and the arts, although quite a few are drawn to medicine—you know, most of our doctors are women. There is always at least one girl who wants to become an actress, and many would like to work in some aspect of the theater.

> *Yuri is also seventeen and just out of high school, and is about to take the entrance exams for a medical institute. He comes from a large, outgoing, and unpretentious family. His great-grandparents were active in one of the first "Soviets"—the councils of government—formed after the Revolution of 1917, and his grandparents still reflect the yeasty Communist spirit of the 1920's. From his family Yuri draws stability and a sense of being in the mainstream of Soviet life.*

In my school there used to be a lot of irritation between teachers and pupils, and once a teacher proposed a composition on the theme, "What do you honestly think of your teachers?" She told us to be very frank, because if the teachers knew precisely what bothered us, perhaps it might lead to some improvements. One boy promptly stood up and said, "I am not going to write on that subject, because if I say what I really think and feel, all of you will be offended, and no matter how good your intentions are now, you will soon begin to dislike me and take it out on me, and, of course, my record will suffer." The teacher thought this over for a moment and said, "I guess you are right." And she withdrew the theme. Since then, some young teachers have come to our school, and relations with them are not bad. The young ones are more patient and willing to come down to our level; they are closer to us.

In my class only one person was not a member of the Komsomol, and he was a poor student, which is why the Komsomol did not accept him. Once a month we had a general Komsomol meeting of the whole school and twice a month there were meetings in each class to talk about how people were doing in their studies and how the community service work was being carried out. About four times a year we had *subbotniki*—Saturdays of volunteer work around the school and community. Another thing the Komsomol members do

Informal discussion in a Leningrad classroom. The bulletin board in the background commemorates Lenin's 100th birthday in 1970. (*Novosti*)

is to look after the younger ones in the school, organizing sports teams, games, and other activities for them. But the Komsomol's main emphasis in school is on our studies.

In our school we started a student group responsible for keeping the class informed on current events, both foreign and domestic. Those of us who were in the group had to read the press thoroughly and gather information and organize it for presentation once a week. I was the head of the group for a while, and I enjoyed it, but it was a lot of extra work for me because I took it seriously. Some of the reporting that we did to our classmates was about what the students abroad are up to. We follow this with interest, but we don't feel ourselves to be a part of this Western student movement or feel that what they are agitated about has much relation to our lives. Perhaps it is too soon for us to feel this.

After the invasion of Czechoslovakia, the teachers gave several talks on the subject. We listened, but there was no discussion with the teachers afterward. And there was not much outward reaction among the students in my school to the trials of the writers here [meaning the trials of Sinyavsky and Daniel and other writers for criticizing the government in the past few years]. For one thing, the school keeps us so busy. Our work load is heavy, and there just isn't much time for other things.

When we do have free time, we read detective stories probably more than any other kind of literature. We read *Yunost*, where the young writers try out their strength. I cannot say that any brilliant ones have appeared in recent years, but the authors published there do show in their stories that they know the mood of the youth pretty well. A lot of us have read Salinger's *Catcher in the Rye* and Hemingway's works, and when we were younger we read Jules Verne and Jack London. Right now, Mark Twain is my favorite Western writer.

We have no ideal figures and no heroes, and our main preoccupation is to criticize those that exist. If there is ad-miration for anyone, it is more apt to be for some of the scientists—for example, Kurchatov [a pioneer nuclear physi-cist who died in 1960].

People here want most of all to travel and see the world. We would go anywhere, to any foreign country, if they would only let us go. Since our traveling has to be at home, we try to pick the most interesting places in the Soviet Union. The Baltic republics attract many of us, because they are more European in look and feeling than almost any other part of the country. Siberia has a different kind of appeal and for some young people. It is a romantic appeal.

Quite a few of my classmates want to become doctors—they just happen to be mostly boys [about 70 per cent of the country's doctors are women]. The girls in my class are at-tracted to teaching. Biology, biochemistry and biophysics are becoming more appealing, physics and chemistry perhaps less so. Before, it was hard to get into the departments of physics and chemistry and relatively easy to stay once you got in. Now I hear that it is easier to get in and harder to stay in—at least, that is what people are saying.

> *Zoya will soon be nineteen. After finishing school she worked at a simple job in a drafting office and is now preparing to go on with her studies full time. Her father is a high-ranking military official, and her family is very well off, with a comfortable apartment in Moscow and a country dacha provided by the government. A grownup who knows her well said, "I always knew that Zoya had intelligence, but now she is beginning to use it—she has really come to life in the past year, since she left school and became more in-dependent of her family."*

There is a big difference between those who finish

school and don't intend to study any more and those of us who are preparing to go on to an institute or to the university. Our interests are quite separate, and I can speak only about the people in the second group, like myself. I am going to study languages. The girls I know are drawn to the humanities, partly because they think there is less competition there than in the field of science.

Our tenth graders are very romantic—they are not at all materialistic at that age. One reason why our students in the university like to go to Siberia to work during the summers at construction projects is because of the comradeship they get there, the chance to live close together in simple surroundings and get to know one another as they cannot during the school year, when everybody is so busy. Besides, it is interesting out there. Sometimes the students get paid for their work and sometimes not, but I think the adventure and the romanticism are more important to them than the money.

In history, our textbooks are very poor, everything is cut and dried, and in my class there was never any discussion between us and the teacher. There was some discussion in literature—after all, people are bound to have different opinions about the literary works they read. Once we were asked to write a paper about Tatiana in Pushkin's *Eugene Onegin*. The teacher was very high on Tatiana—we knew so from everything she had said—but one of the girls in the class disliked that character in the poem and wrote a sharp criticism of her. It was well written, so the teacher gave her an "excellent," but she added the comment, "You should also take the views of adults into consideration." A lot of people just read what is assigned in school. Among those who read widely on their own, our poets Voznesensky and Yevtushenko are quite popular.

Music from the West has an influence on a great many people here. The deeper influences from over there, the political ones, are felt by only a small number of people—some of the writers, people in the universities and scientific institutes, and a few youngsters in high school.

At home and everywhere else we get the message that our parents worked so hard for us and that we ought to be more grateful. Probably this is because they have nothing else to say to us. My mother doesn't understand how I can sit around all day and do nothing. Whenever she sees me I seem to be daydreaming or reading for pleasure, and she thinks I am simply unable to work, which worries her. It is partly that school has been boring for me and I haven't wanted to work. Now I am interested in foreign languages, and I believe I will do well at them.

Sex life here usually begins after high school, and it is very active in the universities and among young working girls who lead an independent life. Many students marry while they are still undergraduates, and there are quite a few divorces soon after. Contraceptives have been almost non-existent here, but now there are signs that the loop is beginning to come in. We were not given any sex education at all in school, and my classmates were even embarrassed to discuss the human anatomy in biology class. I learned about sex from my friends, beginning at the age of eight, and I think it is bad when this learning comes mostly from rumors and backyard stories.

LOOKING BEYOND ONESELF:

TWO VIEWS

*Here are two fragments of conversation that are
interesting in themselves and in relation to each
other. They suggest one useful way of looking at
people. The first is part of a talk I had with the
poet Andrei Voznesensky; you will note that he
feels the young people of today are very much
in the tradition of the Russian intelligentsia of
the nineteenth and early twentieth centuries. The
second excerpt presents a contrasting view and is
from a conversation in Moscow in which I was
not involved, with a disaffected young man who
works in the arts.*

I think that at all times, for Russian young people,
the least characteristic questions have been those of daily
life, questions limited by some kind of narrow materialistic
compass. Russian youth has always been connected with
the fate of the planet—and now this is particularly characteristic. But I will tell you that in order for a man to do
something for the planet, he must for a while, at one or
another period in his life, go deeply into himself, like a bear
that hibernates a part of the time in order to lead a more
active life during the rest of the time. And the same is true
of a creative personality. I know many of our writers who live

a very active life and then suddenly disappear for three months into the provinces. They do this in order to find themselves, to be born again, and these processes have to take place in private. As for Russian young people, I would say that they have always been linked by every nerve with the whole world and that they have been less for themselves than for the whole world. They have had a particularly self-sacrificing attitude about it.

> *From "Three Young Russians," an interview by the British correspondent John Morgan, in* En- counter, *February, 1968:*

I would like to say this about the younger generation. For the last hundred years of the history of young people in Russia, every new generation has interested itself in something outside of itself—either revolution, or religion, or some special purity in relationships, or something else.

But now, for the first time, the new generation—the generation born about 1945, the "children of victory," as they are called—are interested above all in themselves. And all their force of interest is directed inside themselves, though in the first instance to their external physical appearance. And that is a lot more interesting than the sort of young people who can be led here and there. If you are attracted to some public work, you will be helped in your interest. But if you are interested in something connected with yourself as a person, you will find things much more difficult, and you begin to lose trust in everything. That's how young people of the 1945, '46, and '47 generation look at things. They are not interested in things outside themselves.

A WRITER REFLECTS

In an effort to sort out the different views I had heard in Moscow on Soviet youth, I went to see a thoughtful man I know—a Soviet writer who has written for and about young people for many years—and put to him the question, "What are the distinctive characteristics of this generation?"

In comparison with our generation of the late 1920's, these youngsters today are politically unsteady and less sure of themselves. They hesitate, they waver. I tell my students, "You people are not the 'lost generation' that Hemingway described in his early writings; what you are is a confused generation." The students get a kick out of this, and now they go around the corridors calling themselves "the confused ones." They do it in jest, but there is seriousness about it as well.

I would say that the outstanding quality of these thinking young people is their tremendous passion for truth. If you evade the hard and sensitive questions when you talk with them, if you try to smooth over the rough edges and use clichés, they right away stop believing in you and even listening to you. Part of the reason for their attitude is that the de-Stalinization in our country was not carried out in an intelligent way. It was done primitively, by tearing Stalin down from a great hero to a pygmy all at once. [The de-Stalinization campaign was begun in 1956 with a secret speech by Khrushchev at the Twentieth Party Congress criticizing Joseph Stalin for his brutal methods and serious mistakes. The criticism was muted after several years to prevent it from undermining the Party's authority.] We are a very impetuous people; we go from one extreme to the other. Stalin's biggest mistake was that he wanted to build the most ethical society by using unethical means to get there. He thought you could build the society and then forget about the means. But you cannot forget them. His crimes had an influence on what was yet to come, a poisoning influence. They shook the young people's faith not only in Stalin, but in the ideas of Lenin as well. Now we are celebrating Lenin's hundredth birthday, and from morning until night his name and face are everywhere. We are overdoing it, and I fear this will turn the young people off still further.

Of course, we have a generation gap here—the problem of fathers and sons—and it would be foolish to deny it. It is natural that we have such a gap, because such great changes have come about in our world. Take, for example, the old-time locomotive engine. You can see how it works, how the fuel is transformed into steam, which drives the pistons, which turn the wheels—it is all visible to the eye. Now look at an atomic reactor. It is massive and silent and motionless on the outside, yet inside there is all that tremendous power being generated in ways you cannot see. The young people grasp faster than we do how it works, because they have grown up in this kind of a world, where so much is invisible to the eye. In art and literature as well, there is a lot nowadays that is being communicated between the lines and under the surface, and this is natural, for art is a reflection of the rest of life.

The young people do not like authority of any kind, and that is one reason why there are no heroes at the moment, neither in literature nor in life. At one time they admired the cosmonauts, and the death of Yuri Gagarin [the first man to orbit the earth in a spacecraft] was deeply felt by many people. Pavel Korchagin [Soviet Civil War hero in literature] is still something of a hero for the fifteen-year-olds, but our writers such as Aksenov and Gladilin are afraid to create a new hero, because no one will believe in him—to the young he will seem too crystal-like and monumental for the complexities of our time. This is why no new literary hero has appeared.

The youngsters have been reading the war literature with great interest—the memoirs of the Soviet military leaders that have been coming out here in the last decade, and the novels and stories about World War II by such writers as Bykov, Baklanov, and Bondarev. The young are also drawn to the literature on the village. They want to see into the unseen corners of our country, and they like the tendency of this literature to look at the simple person in the countryside and learn what Soviet life has done to him over the years.

Our students follow what goes on among the young people in the West, but they don't feel a community of interests with them, because our worlds are too different, too far apart. We have arguments here about what the content of courses in the humanities should be, and we have conflicts between individual teachers and students, but there is no student movement in our country and no demand for self-government in your sense.

The leadership of the Komsomol is not yet an intelligent-sia, and this makes for difficulties in its work with the well-educated young people. The Komsomol lost by putting the real interests of our youth outside itself, and even in the Pioneers [organization for children from nine to fourteen] there has been too much ritual, too much saluting and drum-beating. The present head of the Komsomol is a more educated man than the last one, so there is at least some hope that the Komsomol will become more responsive to what the young people need and want.

In my talks with people in the Academy of Pedagogical Science, I fight for every hour of the humanities in the school program. The situation is bad: A few years ago they cut down the time devoted to these subjects. The trouble is that there is so much to be learned. Aesthetic education in our schools is very weak; drawing and painting and music are taught in a conventional, even primitive way. People don't think aesthetics are important, at least not enough people do: I too believe that the task of our schools is to teach youngsters

A music class in a traditional school   (*Novosti*)

At one of the special English-language schools in Moscow   (*Novosti*)

to think independently. The sum of knowledge is getting to be so large that you cannot absorb it all; you have to go after what you yourself need to know in life. At one time, Makarenko's influence declined, but now he is on the rise again and his writings will be republished. [Makarenko was a teacher who rehabilitated delinquent and homeless children in the 1920's.] His central message was "trust the child you are bringing up, have confidence in him." One of the things we have learned from our boarding schools is that too much of the collective, of always being and doing things together, is tiring for children. They need to be alone sometimes and to develop independently.

The cover of the magazine *Krokodil*, No. 1, 1969, reflected public interest in the new automobile plant in Togliatti, which produces a Russian version of the Fiat. The baby (*lower left*) is crying, "I want a car," and the mother is saying, "Don't torment the child; buy a Fiat." Three men at the lower right are saying, "A fine car. Maybe we could split it three ways?" This slang phrase is usually applied to a bottle of vodka. The man on the left is wondering if spare parts for another make of car will fit this one. Spare parts are hard to get in Russia.

PART THREE

Attitudes Toward Material Things

What do Russian young people want in the way of material possessions? The same things that youngsters here want? Different things? And how do their material desires compare in force with their nonmaterial aspirations? This is a subject of interest to us, because one of the goals of the Bolshevik Revolution was to redirect people's attitudes toward being part of a Communist society in which they would be motivated by forces other than the desire for material things. The question now is, What has happened in the past fifty years? By and large the Soviet regime has leveled out material possessions to the extent of bringing basic food and housing and other necessities within reach of a large number of people. But to what extent has it succeeded in reshaping people's motivations? Soviet sociologists have been studying consumer desires, including those of youth, and they are just beginning to give us some systematic information on the subject. One group of Moscow young people who were questioned said they aspired to have the fol-

lowing things, in this order: tape recorder, guitar, motorcycle, movie camera, car, piano or accordion, and still camera. This bears out the impression one gets in talking to people that Soviet youngsters who live in the city want pretty much the same things as young urban people elsewhere. There are some differences having to do with cultural tastes: the accordion is a traditional instrument in Russia, yet the striking thing now is how the guitar has won great favor with urban youngsters who listen to a lot of Western jazz and rock music. People's responses are also determined by what is available in the Soviet Union and what is not. A private car is almost totally out of reach for a Soviet teenager, whereas a motorcycle is an immediate possibility. Young people know they are well off when they compare their situation with that of their parents and grandparents, but to the extent they compare it with the outside world, they feel deprived of many things. The important difference from the West is that here affluence is taken for granted, and a segment of the youth is looking restlessly for other values, while in the Soviet Union affluence has not yet arrived, and the desire for consumer goods is very strong.

A GIRL WRESTLES

WITH A PROBLEM

*This letter to the editor is a good curtain-raiser,
because it sets forth in vivid personal terms two
broadly different outlooks toward material things.
One view, expressed by the author of the letter,
is that material possessions can have a corrupting
influence unless you acquire them slowly by your
own hard work. The other point of view, which
the author attributes to her boyfriend, is that
there is nothing wrong with having a lot of things
that you haven't earned—just go ahead and use
and enjoy them. The letter was published in*
Komsomolskaya pravda [Young Communist
League Truth] *under the headline "I Don't Want
to Be Dependent" on January 28, 1969.*

Dear "Komsomolka"!
Please consider this letter personal. I am having a hard
time and I would like your advice. In the Virgin Lands I
got to know a student and we fell in love and decided to
get married. Out there everything was fine. We were all on
an equal plane. Igor was no worse than the others, and for
me he was the best.
It was in Moscow that our disagreements began. I live
with Mama and my sister and brother. My father died a
long time ago. Mother earns very little, but enough, I get

a student stipend, and my little brother is supported by a surviving dependent's pension. We live adequately. I never felt that I was poorer than other people; in fact, I never even thought about that at all.

I didn't know anything about Igor's family. Somehow I did not think about his family's material situation or that it might in some way affect me too.

Now I am having agonizing doubts, and I don't know what to do.

Igor's father earns a lot of money. Igor's room is positively crammed with expensive things: beautiful furniture, rugs, a tape recorder, two record players, two radios, cameras, a photo-enlarger, and a movie camera, and there is even a typewriter (although so far he doesn't need it, but it was bought a long time ago). In short, his room has all the equipment needed to enable a modern, stylish young man to shine among his friends.

Igor is accustomed to living on his father's money, and he plans to go on living that way after he is married. He intends to have a family and to place the material burden of it on his father.

Igor's parents received me warmly, and they are willing to have us live with them. I keep wondering if they don't think of me as a new plaything that they must give to their dear son, since they have never denied him anything and are accustomed to granting his every wish.

I would like to begin life with him not this way, not in these conditions, where everything is provided, but the way my parents began their life together.

Those years were hard. When they got married, they rented a room somewhere; they didn't want to crowd either his parents or hers. They bought an old bed, and Papa himself made a table. We still have the table in our kitchen: Mama wouldn't for anything part with this witness to the beginning of their happy life together. That was how they began life—on their own, and not dependent on somebody's parents.

Igor cannot understand me. He is accustomed to receiving things even before he begins to desire them or, in any case, as soon as he desires them.

I would like to begin life with him out from under guardianship, and with the material means that we ourselves will have. And I would not like Igor to bring to our new life all those expensive things that surround him even though he did not earn them. Then together we will have the pleasure, gradually and in accord with our means, of acquiring everything we need. In general, I don't consider essential to life and happiness the presence of a lot of expensive possessions, especially ones that you have not earned yourself.

Igor has an entirely different opinion. He thinks I am a dreamer and an idealist, that there is no reason to create artificial difficulties for oneself, that just as he now lives with his parents free of care, so the two of us will live with them in a carefree way.

In the end, I don't know whether I'm right or not. Maybe I really do complicate things too much, as Igor says. Should I perhaps give in?

So I have written to you, dear "Komsomolka."—Nina T., Moscow

TONYECHKA (A SONG)

A boy abandons his girl in favor of another whose father has a high establishment position and all the privileges and material comforts that go with it. These are the harsh lyrics of an "underground" song by Alexander Galich—one of the best of Russia's poet-minstrels, whose ballads and songs circulate unofficially through tape recordings.

She gathered up her things and said in a small voice:
"As for your falling in love with Tonka, well, she has nothing
   to do with it!
It's not Tonka's moist lips that seduced you,
But the fact that her papa has a bodyguard assigned to him.
That her Papa has a dacha in Pavshino,
That Papa is surrounded by toadies with secretaries,
That Papa has access to the Central Committee privilege
   shops,
And that on holidays there are movies starring Tselikovskaya!
Your Tonka is too ugly for words—
But don't listen to me, I belong to the past!
And now you're going to sleep with a washboard,
For the sake of her private car. . . .

    That's what you wanted, and you know it yourself.
    You know it, but you're embarrassed.

Over and again you talk about love, about trust,
About lofty things!
But in your mind's eye you see—the dacha in Pavshino,
The bodyguard and the toadies with secretaries,
And how you will watch movies at home with the family,
And happiness will be a caramel on your tongue."

I now live in a house where nothing is lacking,
Even my trousers have zippers,
The wine flows in our home as from a well,
And we have an indoor toilet—eight by ten.
Papasha himself gets home by midnight,
The bodyguards and the toadies all stand at attention!
I pour out 200 grams of vodka for Papasha,
And tell him a joke about the Jews!
But when I go to bed with this idiot, this Tonka,
I remember that other sweet voice.
What a temper that girl has—downright violent,
I telephone her and she hangs up.
Drive me to Ostankino, chief,
To Ostankino, where the Titan movie theater is,
She works there as a ticket taker,
Stands in the entryway, all frozen,
Freezing and shivering,
But she has overcome her love,
Chilled to the bone and grown cold,
But uncompromising and unforgiving.

SOME YOUNG PEOPLE'S GOALS

In 1966 a detailed study was made of 2,204 young people in Leningrad between the ages of seventeen and thirty to find out about their attitudes and goals. Slightly more than half of them were factory workers in various branches of industry, and the rest were engineers, technicians, and students in the institutes and the university. They were not required to sign their names to the questionnaire, but about one-fifth of them did. The interesting thing in the responses is how many of the young people say that they seek an interesting job and a higher education, with the desires for good housing and material prosperity coming third and fourth under the heading of primary goals. These and other results of the survey came out in 1969 in a booklet entitled Young People: About Themselves and Their Contemporaries.

It is interesting to compare this chart with the attitude expressed by some young workers in a factory in Moscow.

Here is the philosophizing of the youngsters at the Likhachev Plant: "Why torture myself studying, when my grandfather didn't finish even two grades, and look how well he lives;" "I want to get into a construction battalion in the army: When I come back I'll have money and I'll get some smart clothes."

YOUNG PEOPLE'S GOALS IN LIFE	Primary Goal %	Secondary Goal %	Total Number of Answers	% of the 2,204 Questioned
To find an interesting job that you like	89.4	10.6	1,339	60.6
To get a higher educa-tion	82.4	17.6	1,357	59.7
To visit other countries	38.8	61.2	1,269	57.5
To achieve material prosperity	69.9	30.1	1,209	54.9
To get good housing	72.7	27.3	1,202	54.6
To improve your profes-sional skills	81.5	18.5	965	43.7
To find true friends	88.1	11.9	951	43.2
To raise your children to be genuine people	80.6	19.4	921	41.8
To meet the one you love	72.9	27.1	916	41.5
To get married	39.0	61.0	705	32.0
To buy a car	32.8	67.2	693	31.4
To complete high school	85.4	14.6	487	22.0
To get work at one of the construction projects	34.6	65.4	405	18.4

ARE SOME PARENTS

OVERDOING IT?

On the subject of material things, Soviet adults and parents harbor mixed feelings toward the young generation. They themselves grew up in hard times and have reached a more comfortable standard of living only in middle age or later. It is natural for them to want to share their benefits with their children; they derive real enjoyment out of bringing home to them the new toys and consumer goods that come on the Soviet market. Yet there is also a feeling of resentment, that things come too easily to the young these days. As one writer has put it, "An inflation of material values for adolescents, as it were, is taking place before our eyes." The whole range of feelings is present in these two articles from Pravda. The first, published on June 19, 1969, is about urban youngsters at graduation time; the second, dated January 22, 1967, gives a characteristic view of a peasant family's attitude.

I remember how a family I know well prepared for their daughter's graduation festivities. After visiting a dozen stores in a futile quest for something "bright, youthful, and springlike," the mother—somewhat to her own surprise—bought a bridal outfit: an airy, ruffled dress and bridal veil

("It will soon come in handy," the salesgirl assured the mother prophetically). She paid forty-seven rubles, eighty-six kopeks for the outfit.

The grandmother held a place in the queue at the hairdresser's from 6 A.M. She couldn't sleep anyway. After the girl's hair was done, the girl returned home about two in the afternoon with a headache and obviously the wrong kind of bangs. Some tears and despair, a pinch of patience, ten drops of menthol valerate (for mother), a tiny bit of lacquer, and the hairdo finally looked fashionable.

They went to the school early, around five. But alas, no one was smitten by Marina's appearance. Her girl friends' dresses were resplendent with gold filament, beads and sequins and their heads were crowned by "towers," "decorative braids," "fantasies" and other hairdos. These weren't girls, they were New Year's trees. They awaited the photographer for an hour and had their pictures taken for an hour—in one group, individually, and in smaller groups. The homeroom teacher had announced earlier that there would be no alcohol at the party. The warning had an "effect": some boys' pockets bulged suspiciously.

Later, in the auditorium, after the solemn valedictory speech and the salutitarian's response, everyone was given a diploma to the sound of an orchestral flourish, only to have the diplomas gently taken back a few minutes later: Something still had to be filled in.

But now representatives of the parents' committee (other fathers and mothers were not invited) called everyone to the table. It was crammed with dainty appetizers and mountains of market strawberries. Supper passed in awkward silence.

Dancing started. The girls, as is the custom, were shy at first, but many boys were not. At the table, meanwhile, sat tragedy personified: In rising from his chair a boy had spilled a dish of strawberry juice onto the dress of the classmate sitting next to him. The parents' committee sprinkled salt all over the right side of the girl's dress, while she choked on her tears and kept saying, "My mother will die!"

It is possible that I have laid it on rather too thick in places. But essentially everything happened exactly this way. A million worries over outfit, hairdo, the festive table, and in the end, boredom and disappointment. To judge by the "traditional" July letters to the editors, this by no means happens only in Marina's school.

Let's not be hypocrites. Let's not force seventeen-year-olds into an afternoon graduation party with packaged candy and pear-flavored drinks. We should not content ourselves with the fact that *in our time* we were satisfied with our sister's well-worn dress while secretly envying our girl friend's new one of serge lining material. *Their time* can hardly be compared with ours. Since everything we do is ultimately directed to making our children's lives better, we should go forward, as they say, from where we are. And yet—

It is extremely interesting for me, for example, to understand the psychology of a tenth grader who gives her parents an ultimatum: "Either a white lace dress over nylon, or I won't go to the party!" What gives rise to superdemands from a person who has not yet reached her majority and has not earned a single kopek? The increasing family income, considerations of prestige, the inexorable laws of fashion? Probably all three.

Four people sat around the table in a big, spacious room: Ivan Tikhonovich's wife, a young and jolly woman who is a bookkeeper at a dairy-products section; the man of the house; the school director; and I.

"We have three children," Maria Fyodorovna said, speaking in a pleasant provincial accent. "Kolya [Nikolai], the oldest, is in the tenth grade. Nyusya is in the eighth grade, and Lenochka has just started school."

"You ask whether we love our children. How can one help

loving them? We are not old, we live only for our children, there is nothing we wouldn't do for them. Obviously, we want them to be successful."

"Successful, you say! What do you mean by 'successful'?"

Our host thought for a minute:

"Well, Nikolai will go to an agricultural institute. That's been decided. Later he can go into the brigade and work in the same job as his grandfather. My father was a first-class blacksmith. He was famous throughout the neighborhood. Before he died last year, he said Nikolai should work with iron but not lose touch with the land. And he isn't losing touch, he heads the school brigade."

"Nyusya has decided to be a doctor, and if she can't get into the institute, she wants to be a feldsher [a doctor's assis-

Window shopping

tant]," our hostess broke into the conversation, as if voicing a dream.

"You said there's nothing you wouldn't do for your children. Tell me, how does this concern manifest itself?"

"Well, you know how things are. People have become more cultured now, in the cities and in the countryside too. In my time, my mother used to alter one of her homemade skirts or make cotton blouses herself, and this was our entire wardrobe."

"Yes, times have changed." Ivan Tikhonovich rubbed his chin. "How much did you take to Syzran the other day?"

"What's the point of counting it when it's for your children?" Maria Fyodorovna began enumerating her purchases in a dignified manner. "We bought an overcoat for Kolenka, a suit, three shirts, a pair of boots."

"With pointed toes." Grandmother, who had been sitting quietly in a corner, could not help breaking in. "He wanted boots with pointed toes. And we've spent more than 110 rubles on little Nyusenka; we bought her a scarf in Orenburg and shoes."

And before our host had time to open his mouth, there was the click of a lock, a heavy lid was lifted and the fine apparel that had been purchased for the children was extracted from the interior of a huge trunk.

It is not by chance that I have told in such detail about my meeting with the parents of schoolchildren in a Volga-area village. In many families the adults, out of love for their offspring, deprive themselves of articles of prime necessity and buy luxuries for the children, often spending almost their entire earnings on such purchases.

THE MATERIAL SIDE OF

UNIVERSITY LIFE

University students are a group somewhat apart in their outlook and needs—although not as much as people tend to think, according to a thoughtful article by Valery Agranovsky, a journalist who spent time observing and talking with students at the university in Gorky. Here is part of his article, which appeared in the magazine Yunost (Youth), *No. 12, 1967.*

I put 10,000 rubles in brand-new notes into each of twenty-five envelopes, distributed them to twenty-five students as if I were Croesus, and said, "Spend it!" It was just a game, but only two of them managed to work their way through the whole amount, and then only because they got the idea of buying a Volga car, although it seems to me that a motorcycle would be more suitable for a student. The other spendthrifts and squanderers, having spent not even half of their money, finally gave up.

Here is how one girl—an inveterate tourist—used her 10,000 rubles. First of all, she bought hiking and camping equipment, starting with a tent and ending with heavy winter clothing, and with two friends went off to roam around Kamchatka [a peninsula in the Soviet Far East]. Naturally, she footed the whole bill for her friends. Upon returning, she immediately set out for Spain, which she had dreamed of seeing ever since, as a child, she read the writings of Koltsov [a Soviet war correspondent in the Spanish Civil War]. Then, really pushing her impetuous fantasy, she bought a bicycle. And that was all. We added it all up very carefully and found out that she had spent 4,100 rubles. I knew this girl had one best dress and three everyday dresses, four woolen sweaters ("My sister and I share them," she said), and three pairs of shoes, one of them winter shoes. "Is your stipend adequate for you?" "Of course not!" and her eyes became very round. But in spite of her eyes, I understood that with such requirements as this girl has, one can manage to get along.

When I asked Lebedev how he would start spending the 10,000, he did not hesitate for a second and answered, "First I would announce to everyone that I have some 'mad' money." This means that the whole class gets invited to a banquet in a restaurant. Then Lebedev would buy his mother a washing machine with a spinner, his father "whatever he desires," some presents for his relatives, and books for himself. Then he would go and visit some foreign country— France, for example—taking with him a certain girl who is a third-year student at the university. "That would cost you twice as much," I remarked. "Three times as much," Lebedev quietly corrected me without so much as moving a muscle. We could not calculate his expenditures: Just try and predict the appetite of his classmates, his father's desire, and the Parisian whims of Lebedev's female companion. Filthy lucre was not given to man for counting.

I stayed in Gorky for about a month, and that whole time, whenever I saw him, Lebedev was always wearing the same green suit. He wore it to class, he lay on the bed in it—if his mother wasn't watching—and he would have worn it to the banquet in the restaurant too. Besides this, he had a winter coat, which that same student girl friend of his said was "terrible looking," a gray lightweight coat for spring and fall, a couple of sweaters, and some small things—shirts, socks, one tie, and a pair of shoes, size 45, which must be the ones referred to in the student song that goes, "One pair of *bashmaki* will last me until I die." This was the wardrobe of our friend to whom money meant nothing.

Of course, Lebedev is somewhat old-fashioned: For him, the cult of the mind has clear priority over the cult of clothes. Still, the general rise in the standard of living is naturally also reflected among the students, who have begun to dress quite presentably and even fashionably. It's all very easy for students to make the grand gesture of saying, "Well, since we are students, we don't need material possessions." But they do need them! Make no mistake about that. It is another question whether they have the money to buy the things they need. I met a first-year girl who spent her stipend on a pair of high-fashion shoes for twenty-seven rubles and then for the next four days, until her parents responded to an urgent request for replenishment, subsisted on thirty kopeks a day: salad, tea, and the indispensable pastry.

Of what is a student's income composed? First of all, it depends on the earnings of his parents. Lebedev's father, a retired soldier, makes two hundred thirty rubles a month, which includes his pension. His mother gets ninety rubles a month. There are four in the family, so, as Lebedev says, it breaks down to eighty rubles "per nose." According to university regulations, a student from such a well-off family is eligible for a stipend only if there are no "threes" [minimum passing grades] on his academic record. If his family's income is more than eighty rubles per person, a student has to get "five" [maximum grade] in all courses to qualify for a stipend; if the family earnings are below sixty rubles per person, then a student can have "threes" and still qualify All of these gradations are determined each year by the university itself, by its special commission (which for some reason has no student representatives, as is the practice in some institutions of higher learning in our country). It decides according to the size of the stipend fund allocated by the ministry and according to its own predictions of how well the students will do in their studies. It is very difficult to guess precisely how the students will do, and the university bookkeeper's heart bleeds when he has to return unspent funds to the Ministry of Finance.

One cannot say that stipends are a key factor in student success, since the whole stipend policy has its sharp edge pointing backward (it punishes past sins) rather than forward (it does not stimulate future achievement). A student can study like a fiend for a whole semester, but it is precisely during this hard period that he gets no money because of the "two" [failing grade] he received in one of his courses the year before.

You also cannot say that a stipend is the subsistence minimum, because not everybody gets one. Moreover, I sense here a kind of wage-leveling turned inside out: A situation is possible where two students with equal ability and equal achievement in their studies are in an unequal position with regard to stipend, which, as we have seen, depends on the income of the parents. And it is far from clear whether the parents will share their income with their offspring and in what amounts they will share it.

In my view, a stipend should be regarded as first of all a subsistence minimum and secondarily as a stimulus to study. This would be humane, at the very least. If a worker does not fulfill the plan, he still gets paid some wages. If a student is not expelled for poor grades and is allowed to stay at the university, he should not be deprived of his stipend.

For two semesters out of six, our Lebedev went regularly to the university cashier's window; the rest of the time his mother was his cashier. There was no spoiling him at home; they gave him just enough money to cover his bus fare and his midday meal, and before each trip to the movies he would say to his mother, "Ma, how about a check for one million?" He smoked Northern cigarettes, did not drink vodka, lived modestly, and seldom went to the savings bank. With the money he earned in the Virgin Lands, he made only one independent purchase, and that was not for himself but for his father. He bought him a fur-lined Siberian coat, although no one could understand why his father would need such a coat if he did not work as an outdoor watchman.

The students who come to Gorky from other cities keep house for themselves. Some of them (the majority) receive money from their parents each month—fifteen to twenty rubles to supplement their stipend, and if they have no stipend, they receive the whole sixty rubles from their parents. Some students live on their stipend alone—forty-five rubles a month in the radiophysics faculty. (In other faculties it is even less, but we are somehow accustomed to the notion that students should be poor.) As a rule, the money all goes for food, calculating one ruble, twenty kopeks to one ruble, forty kopeks a day. The little that remains is spent on cigarettes, books, and recreation.

Many students work to earn additional money. There was a time when they were ashamed to say so, although there is nothing in it to be ashamed of! It is a sin not to make use of an army of young people who represent a great intellectual force. Unfortunately, so far, no one can find the right application for this force. Students find jobs as night watchmen, firemen, truck drivers; strangely enough, almost no one uses his own special knowledge to earn an extra ruble and do some skilled good for the society.

PART FOUR

Scenes from the Life of a Young Worker

These are some excerpts from the scenario for the movie Three Days in the Life of Viktor Chernyshev *by E. Grigoryev, which appeared in the late 1960's. It is about a nineteen-year-old boy who lives in Moscow and works as a lathe operator in a factory. He goes by the nicknames Vitka and Vitya. The movie shows what his daily routine is like, who his friends are and how they spend their free time, and what his thoughts, feelings, and expectations of life are. There was a controversy in the Soviet press about the film. Some critics thought it too negative a picture. I believe it gives a very vivid and accurate portrayal of the life of a large segment of young Soviet workers. The script was published in the Soviet magazine* Isskustvo kino (Art of Film), *No. 5, 1967.*

1. THE USUAL

"Get up, get up, get up,"—like a commander's order. It's the mother rousing her son.

And here he is already at the table having breakfast with his sister's husband, and his mother is serving them: This means she keeps moving between the stove (they are eating in the kitchen) and the table and cupboard, and the whole time she is serving and clearing away. Everything is silent except for the radio, which is transmitting "the latest news" in a startlingly loud voice. It is reporting international developments. "In Holland a jet fighter plane crashed and the pilot was killed." The brother-in-law listens with a look of gloomy concentration, and with the same concentration he butters his bread thickly and eats it, biting off each piece emphatically and looking straight ahead all the while. And then he says to Vitka, "They say the price of beer is going to go down. Have you heard?"

"Which beer?" Vitka asks gravely.

"All beer."

"No," says Vitka gravely, "I haven't heard."

They continue eating and looking straight ahead, the mother moves about, and the radio goes on reporting.

Now Vitka, his jacket on, is running down the stairs.

He starts to dash across the street, then all around him there are cars moving, and he calmly comes to a standstill and looks right past them (this is almost symbolic). The cars, calmly and without panic—this one is an experienced pedestrian, you can live with that kind—skirt around him, and then Vitka makes another dash forward.

Now he is at the bus stop, the trolleybus comes up, and the whole line of people, their attention fixed, compresses itself, becomes elastic and squeezes into the trolleybus.

It is crowded on the bus, people press in on Vitka and turn him around so that he is riding backward, and he grabs hold of the upper crossbar. "Hold onto the air," people joke in a quiet way.

They tumble out of the bus and start walking, shaking themselves out and glancing back at their "dear bus," and they go forward in somber concentration. Suddenly they all smile at once and raise their hands in greeting: "Hi! Hello!" And they go on walking with that solemn and concentrated look.

And once more: "Greetings! Hello!"

And again they are solemn.

Then the revolving door of the entrance way, and here we don't see Vitka—he is lost among the others.

He punches the time clock.

Then he changes his clothes in the locker room. They all stand around by their lockers throwing out remarks to no one in particular. In the shop a radio is on, still going over "the latest news."

Vitka comes out of the locker room, passes under the clock into the shop, takes his place at his machine, nods to one person, smiles to another. Someone has turned off the radio, there is a moment of silence, then a siren sounds, and, making haste while it wails, the machines come to life.

Vitka Chernyshev sleeps. He smiles in his sleep. He is preparing for the day.

"Get up," his mother says. "Get up, Vitya, get up, get up," and she begins to shake him.

"All right," says Vitka, his eyes still closed. "I am getting up. I am."

Breakfast. Vitka with his brother-in-law Kolya, and his mother doing the serving. The radio isn't asleep either, it is reporting on Algeria. Kolya butters his bread and starts eating it.

"I hear they're going to lower prices before the holidays—have you heard?" says Vitka.

"They ought to," Kolya readily agrees, with the age-old hopefulness of simple folk. And again they eat in silence. The radio reports a Negro demonstration in America.

"They set dogs on them," says Kolya.

"Yeah," says Vitka.

Then Vitka runs down the stairs.

He dashes across the street and the cars stream around him.

He climbs onto the bus.

Then the getting out and the "Hi! Hello!"

And the factory entrance hall.

The revolving door.

The courtyard.

The shop.

The time clock.

The locker room and the radio.

Walking under the clock.

Chernyshev stands at his machine, his attention fixed. The radio suddenly stops. He turns on the machine, and just then the siren wails and another working day begins.

2. CHERNYSHEV CLOSE UP

Vitka is standing alone. Alone over his machine, but we don't see the machine, we see only him bending over his work, his face humane and fine-looking as it is absorbed in creating something. Let the camera pause here, let us leave the bustle on all sides and take a good look at him, and the music will assist us. We'll stay with him until he finishes this piece of work. He will no longer be smiling his standard smile: He doesn't need it now.

"Hello!"

Vitya raises and lowers his eyes.

"How are things?"

Vitya again glances up for a second.

"Good for you." The voice is approving. "That's the way to work." The tone of the voice changes. "Tomorrow we're having a *voskresnik* [a Sunday of unpaid volunteer work]. We're going out to dig potatoes. From our group, you, Kuleshov, Razorenov, and Stepan Yegorich are going."

Vitya is silent—after all, he is working.

"That's the situation." Silence. "Is it okay with you?"

Vitya nods.

"Be at the main entrance at seven-thirty in the morning. I've checked off your name. Be sure to come. Don't let me down. I've checked you off."

Vitya nods and gives him a squinting glance as he leaves. He is alone again.

"Chernyshev?"

"That's me." Vitya smiles.

"Viktor?" The old man's eyes narrow as he peers through his glasses.

"Right you are." He smiles again. "Hello, Vasil Zakharych."

"Good morning," the other says more gently. "How is your work going?"

"It's going well."

"That's good," says the strict Vasil Zakharych.

Vitka nods in agreement. And they are silent. Then Vitka sighs as if someone has died. "Spartak, Vasil Zakharych?" Vitka's eyes grow sad and moist; he shakes his head with a distressed, expectant look. "What's happened to them, eh?" [Spartak is a leading Moscow soccer team.]

Vasil Zakharych loses no time in answering. "What about Spartak?" he replies severely. "Let them all go to work. Every one of them. And that's that! They've had it too good, the parasites."

Vitka also acts indignant and supports him. "To the mines, send them down into the mines. For a ten-hour shift."

"To dig with a shovel for ten hours. Ten hours!" repeats Vasil Zakharych vindictively (he is a man of principle, all right). "And no more trips abroad for them. None whatsoever. Enough of that!"

"It can't be ten hours. In the mines they work less than that."

"Well, we can make those parasites work ten hours. By special decree at the request of the working people, to jolt their stomachs. Say, are you contributing any money?"

Vitka is almost a veteran worker, but even he is not accustomed to such quick transitions. "Money for what?"

"Serebryakov is retiring."

"For Uncle Pasha? Why, of course."

"Here is the list. Shall I put you down?"

"Put me down, put me down. Does this mean an invitation?"

"For those who give money," Vasil Zakharych says crossly. The old man doesn't like muddle-headed fellows.

"Oh-h-h." Vitka finally catches on. "How much is everyone contributing?"

"It depends on how decent a person is." And he begins to rustle the paper. "Some give a ruble, and some only twenty kopeks—Alexandrov, for example."

"What a pig," Vitka, of course, agrees, "and an activist, too. When are you going to kick him out of the Party?" He looks toward the back of the shop where Alexandrov is standing, the one who put him down for Sunday's work.

"Why kick him out of the Party?" Vasil Zakharych looks surprised. "He's a good fellow. It's just that he's greedy. 'Out of the Party'!—you people think you're so smart, don't you. Listen, everybody has shortcomings."

"All right, he's a good fellow—then leave him in. Have I said anything against it? Say, what are most people contributing?"

"Most people are giving fifty kopeks."

Young workers leaving the gate of a large factory in Leningrad

"I'll do what everybody is doing, why should I get out of line, am I any better than the others? As everyone does, so will I—we live in a collective, after all. Isn't that right, Vasil Zakharych?"

"Right," mutters that one with satisfaction. "I'll put you down. Fifty kopeks. Chernyshev. There you are."

"Uh-huh," confirmed Vitka, "Chernyshev, fifty kopeks. 'Like money in the bank.' Do I have to sign my name?"

"Ha-ha," Vasil Zakharych loves a joke. He smiles. "Go ahead, sign your name, let's be bureaucratic." Then, again in a stern voice, to finish up the conversation, "You're right. Go ahead and joke about it. It's better to joke than not to, that's the way life is. Better to joke about it. Make fun of it, go ahead and make fun—I won't stop you."

Vitka follows him with his eyes and then goes back to his work and his thoughts.

"What's the matter, Viktor, been chattering?"

"What do you mean?"

"Let's get on with the work!" the foreman growls. He is never satisfied. When a man has that kind of character, you can't change him. "Get on with the plan and do your talking afterward."

"I am, I am, Ivan Petrovich. Look at all I've done!" and he nods to the side.

"Okay now, come on, come on."

"You don't have to tell us, we understand—we finished the tenth grade."

Again Viktor is alone and smiling at his own thoughts. And frowning, too.

A fellow of Vitya's age comes by, looking preoccupied. This time it is Chernyshev who stops him. "How are things?"

"So-so. And with you?" Then, with hope in his voice, "Will you run for our shop tomorrow?"

"Where to?"

"Five kilometers, cross country."

"Are you crazy? Five kilometers! That's a long way! And I've never done any running!"

"Never done any? Well, now you will. I'll put you down."

"Go ahead, put me down, only I'm already signed up to dig potatoes."

"Dig potatoes?"

"You heard me."

Finally, right from the heart: "I'm sick and tired of it all. This one can't do it and that one can't. This one is going to dig potatoes, that one turnips. What am I supposed to do? Knock myself out more than anyone else?"

Vitka comes to his support. "You're absolutely right. There's no order in this world." But the other fellow has already turned away.

Vitka is upset for the fellow. He shakes his head and even tosses a comment to his neighbor. "It's hard work being an enthusiast!"

"Hello, Vitya."

"Hi, Uncle Sash." And, of course, he inquires, "How are things?"

"So-so," Uncle Sasha sighs. "We're going to a funeral tomorrow."

"That's bad," Vitka puts it precisely. "Whose funeral?"

"Just a second, I'll tell you." And he reads from a sheet of paper, "Osmolovsky, Vyacheslav Edmundovich."

"Who's that?"

"A deserving man, an Old Bolshevik. Gave his whole life to the Party, naturally. Tomorrow, be at the subway entrance at eleven o'clock—we're going to lay a wreath. We'll go and pay him a final tribute and be done by noon. Even earlier. There's nothing to it—just a walk—that's all."

"Why do they have to do it on Sunday? They could do it today. They could let us off from work for as long as they need. Or put the whole thing off till Monday."

"They already talked about that in the Party committee.

But you can't take account of everything. I'm checking off your name. Be at the subway at eleven o'clock. Remember, we have to pay our last respects."

"Of course we have to. But Uncle Sash, I— ah— we're going to dig potatoes tomorrow."

"Dig potatoes? They've already put you down for that?"

"Well, of course," Vitka nods. "Paper doesn't tell a lie, now, does it?"

"No, it doesn't," Uncle Sasha says with some despair. "Look at the mess we end up with—what a life! Okay, go back to work, I won't bother you any more." And off he goes.

And Vitka is left alone. He is finishing up. For the first time we see on camera how he works at his lathe with strained attention. Now he is done. He turns off the machine and lays the finished part next to the others he made that day. He looks them over, and we too see them for the first time—the results of his day's work.

3. ON THE STREET CORNER

On the street corner near the apartment house, in all kinds of weather, stand the young "eagles," taking turns like sentries. They stand and look about them. Four of them are there now: Kolya, a twenty-three-year-old lad, with a stylish haircut, wearing gloves and sunglasses, although the sky is overcast; Mishka, a student at the Moscow Aviation Institute, the only son of "respectable parents"; Vovka Sukharev, called "Sukhar," who runs the projector in the local movie theater; and the fourth is Seryoga, a thirteen-year-old kid.

They are talking about something. Then Sukhar begins to demonstrate the more extreme techniques of heavyweight wrestling, which he apparently saw in a movie. He and Mishka begin to wrestle. Kolya glances down the street and then stops them. They all smile broadly. "Go ahead, Sukhar," Kolya says.

And Sukhar, with great virtuosity, gives forth an imbecilic neighing laugh that resounds over the whole street.

Vitka is approaching them. Without stopping he answers with a similar neighing. The whole gang breaks up laughing, then suddenly falls silent. The silence becomes oppressive. All you can hear is the sound of high heels.

They all look and notice her. She is a goddess, naturally, and they all grow quiet. She goes past them, walking like Christ on the water, and she is out of another world, out of their class.

"Her legs are fat," says Sukhar. "Look how she walks."

"You fool!" says Kolya. "She's de luxe. Real class."

"Marvelous!" Vitka concurs. "Her heels should be a little higher."

"She's a dream!" says Mishka. "Here for a moment and gone. And where are you?"

"But her legs!" Sukhar says once again.

"Her legs," repeats Mishka." What a small-time aesthete you are. You mean that just because she isn't yours, she's bad. Why, those legs deserve to be on display in a museum! You're not dry behind the ears yet!"

They all laugh and abruptly fall silent. Their attention switches to someone else.

4. RELATIVES

Uncle Pavel sits opposite, one-armed, tanned, unshaven, his face all wrinkled, and looks his nephew over. "You've grown. You've grown a lot! You're a city boy, city to the core. Remember me?"

"Of course I do. You bought a radio, remember?"

"Yes," says Uncle Pavel, "It was a good radio." And to Vitka's mother: "Vasili broke it at his wedding, the drunken fool! He's all right otherwise, but when he has a drink he becomes stupid, he begins to tell his life story. Do you remember Vasily?"

"I do."

"He sends you warm greetings. And some presents. He has a baby son, born on Easter, named Kolya."

"Kolya," Vitka repeats.

"I already told your mother, all the Dyomins send greetings too. They wanted to know how you are and what you are doing."

"Thanks. Greetings to them, too."

"Thank you. Your grandfather, Makar Stepanovich, also asked about you, asked when are you finally coming to see him?! I told him you don't have time, you are busy people, you're watching television." He laughs at his own joke. "You are hurting his feelings! You've promised to come so many times!"

"Yes," says Vitka. "We'll come." And to change the subject, "How is grandfather? How's his health?"

"Not so good. He's gotten weak. His health is poor. Most of the time he is silent. You've never seen him, have you?"

"No," Vitka is embarrassed.

"You have no time. And he's too old to come and visit you."

Vitka's mother comes to his rescue. "He works a lot, he has no time, and his vacation came in the winter."

"We all work. Don't worry, if he wanted to come, he'd find the time. Isn't that right?"

"To your health!" Vitka says.

"Thanks. Eat, Vitya, eat. Let's see how strong you are." He feels Vitka's biceps. "Not too bad. You know, it's hard to get into an institute. At home four people took the entrance exams this year and only one got into a tekhnikum. The competition was stiff. Yes, it's hard, all right." He looks at Vitka.

"I didn't even apply."

"Is that so! You were afraid to? How come you're so scared?"

"What is there to be scared of! It's not a matter of fear."

"What is it then?" his uncle asks quickly and tenaciously.

"Well—" Vitka is reluctant. "It makes no difference whether you go to an institute or not!"

"So that's what you think," his uncle says slowly and draws back. "That's how you reason. Well, then, of course." And with inner contempt: "Then of course. Why bother? You're clever enough as it is. Very clever. You're sick and tired of going to school. It doesn't take much to satisfy you— you're not greedy to learn!"

"Take Mitka, for example, and the kind of man he was: He loved a good time. He could talk on any subject for a whole day, for two days, three days, whatever you wanted. Sing? Why of course! He knew how to handle wood—the beautiful wooden spoons he carved—and he was a real fisherman. Then he came to the city. And what do you think? He became a plumber. But there was no more man, he wilted away! Of course, a city is in the center of things: conveniences, theaters, museums, the State Department Store, the Central Department Store. It's all fine, there's no denying it. Just fine— who says it's bad? Money handed to you twice a month at the factory. You've finished your shift, now go pick your nose. Or play dominos. What's bad about that?"

"If it's so bad," says Vitka, "let him go back home and carve spoons."

"Let who go back?"

"What do you mean, who?" Vitka begins to feel uneasy, glancing at the motionless back. "Your Mitka!"

Uncle Pavel swings around. His eyes are big and dark, and a strange smile flickers on his face.

"What do you mean 'your Mitka'?" He looks Vitka up and down. "I'm talking about your father. Your father!" And he takes another hard look at Vitka. "How is it that you don't recognize your own father?" There is a flash of contempt in his voice.

"How could he?" his mother comes to his aid.

"I don't know him," Vitka says and looks at them both with curiosity. He knows that his father was killed—he remembers that. Many fathers did not come back from the front. He loves the person he never knew, if you can call that love.

But for Uncle Pavel, Vitka's father is Mitka, a living person.

5. CHATTER

"We are sportsmen, Soviet athletes. We've just returned from the West, and it's so good to breathe this clean air, to see our simple native birch trees and the green, green grass, and to hear pure Russian names—Natasha, Tanya. We've brought back a few things—stockings! All of Paris is crazy about them, they are all wearing stockings—even Jean Marais."

"You mean you were in Paris?" bursts out one of the girls.

"Yes," declares 'Son.' "Paris is a magnificent city. Have you ever been there?"

"What?"

"Go there, you won't be sorry. It's an amazing city. The whole Russian intelligentsia loved Paris, and the revolutionaries Herzen and Ogaryev and the later ones—they all went through the experience of Paris. Yevtushenko, too. Oh, absolutely, you must go. What a city! All the women are French and everybody speaks French. It's simply amazing. Imagine, organizing a whole place like that!"

"How amusing," says the girl sitting opposite Vitka.

"Very amusing. Very. I'm still surprised myself. Forgive us, we haven't introduced ourselves." 'Son' jumps up and bows gallantly. "Borya and Yura," and he indicates Vitka. "We are two young beginning physicists—students, of course. What are your names?"

The girls are slow to answer. They are put off by Vitka's behavior—sitting there and not saying a word—the worst kind of person for a party.

Finally, hesitatingly, the one sitting opposite 'Son,' who asked about Paris, introduces herself. "Mila," and, indicating her friend, "Inga."

She uncertainly stretches out her hand across the table, and Borya (we'll call him that) automatically, as a Polish officer would do, takes her hand and kisses it. Then, like a swan's wing, another hand stretches out, and it too receives its tribute.

"Are you fond of ballet?" Mila asks.

Tenderness fills Borya's eyes. "I adore it."

"I just love ballet," says Mila, and claps her hands. "Ulanova is a delight."

"And poetry. Right?" Borya falls in with her.

"Fascinating," Mila exclaims. "I can read it all night long."

Suddenly Borya falls silent, he settles back and even closes his eyes in fatigue. And the whole restaurant—the orchestra, the couples dancing, and the people at tables— are all part of the same rhythm, chatter, chatter.

Dancing in a cafe (Novosti)

6. CHERNYSHEV'S AUTOBIOGRAPHY

After a Sunday of potato-digging, Vitka joins his friends, and they stop in a store to buy some bottles of wine for the evening. There is a line at the cashier's booth and the boys are impatient; one of them crashes the line and is challenged by an elderly man who has been patiently waiting his turn: "Do you think you're better than everybody else?" Angered, the boys follow him out of the store. One thing leads to another, and before they know it, they have fallen upon him and beaten him. At the police station, Vitka is interrogated by two young lieutenants.

"Chernyshev, Viktor Dmitrievich. Born in Moscow in 1946. Went to kindergarten. Went to school." Vitka racks his brain to recall something more interesting and important to say.

"Were you a Pioneer?"

"I was. I was a Pioneer. Went to Pioneer camp."

"How many times did you go to camp?"

This takes Vitka by surprise. "Every summer from first grade on. They sent me every year."

"Have you done any community work?"

"Community work? I played soccer. Played the drums. I was in three amateur talent shows. You know, the usual."

"What did you do in the talent shows?"

"I recited poetry," says Chernyshev, unsure of himself. He feels this is all so elementary that it isn't even worth talking about.

"What poetry?"

Chernyshev tries to remember. " 'As soon as you put on the neckerchief—' That was one poem, about a Young Pioneer," he explains. " 'Korea is on fire, we support you—' that was another. This show was for New Year's. And then there was an 'Evening of Humor': 'Step aside, the Soviet ruble is coming—' " He thinks some more, trying hard to remember. "And in sixth grade I was in the play *The Young Guard* [from a famous novel about young underground fighters in World War II]. But that was nothing special."

"What part did you play? Tyulenin?"

"No, a minor part. A Rumanian. They gave me the part, so I played it."

"When did you finish school?

"Year before last."

"Are you in the Komsomol?"

"Yes."

"Have you done any Komsomol work?"

"Just the things everybody does. Giving news reports at meetings, collecting scrap metal, being a Young Pioneer leader."

"You were a Young Pioneer leader, too?"

"Yes. I was. They appointed me one."

"And how did you do?"

"Not badly. I took the kids on a ski trip. We took part in a contest with some others. We went to the Lenin Museum and the Museum of the Revolution, and to the theater. The usual things."

"Did you get any penalties?"

"No."

"Any special mentions of appreciation?"

"No. Only the general ones they give to everybody all at once."

"Were you ever elected to the bureau or the committee [the governing bodies of the Komsomol]?"

"I was nominated, but I didn't get elected."

"And now you work at the factory?"

"Yes."

"As a lathe operator?"

"Yes."

"Do you like your work?"

"It's all right."

"What else do you do?"

"What?"

"What are you interested in? What do you want for yourself?"

"I want—" Chernyshev speaks unsurely. "Same as everyone, what more do I want? There are things that interest me. What are my interests? I go to the movies. I relax. I watch television. Sometimes I do the shopping for my mother, and other things for her. The usual."

"Is that all?"

"Yes."

"Anything else? What do you aspire to in life?"

Chernyshev thinks hard. He is tired of this conversation. Why didn't they punish him right off and be done with it? He waits for the next question, but there isn't any. "What do I aspire to?" Chernyshev is embarrassed, he just cannot think of what he aspires to. Somehow, before now, he has been so busy he has never had time to think about it. "I want the good things," Chernyshev barely gets it out, and blushes again. "Same as everyone," he says once again. Then he closes up.

"It's a short biography. Not much in it."

"What?"

"I say, it doesn't amount to much. 'Same as everyone.'

What have *you* done?" Chernyshev looks dull and confused, he doesn't understand what they want from him.

"I myself? I—" and again he shuts up for good.

"It's not much for a boy who's eighteen. Not much. You thought you could get by without doing anything serious, didn't you? You'd better watch out, boy!"

Chernyshev is silent. He has always been taught to do and be like everyone else. Now life is becoming more complicated.

7. BEGINNING A NEW LIFE

The boys stand silent.

"Hi," Vitka says. They nod to him.

"Say, what was the matter with you?" Mishka looks at Vitka. "You could at least have said something. Spoken out about the problems of youth, turned the militia office into a forum!"

"Stop!" says Sukhar.

"Drop it!" says Vitka.

Mishka looks them over with curiosity. "You're in a bad mood. I'm sorry, I didn't realize. Well, what do you say we start all over?! Let's go to the library."

"Enough, Mishka!" Chernyshev says.

"Ech, you people! How irritable we've become. Youth!" he drags out the word. "The hope of the nation! The Decembrists aroused Herzen, and Herzen aroused the 'raznochintsy' [middle-class intellectuals of the nineteenth century]."

"What shall we do?" Sukhar asks.

"What about going to the movies?"

"Oh, come on, now!"

"Well, what do we do? Where is there to go? You see what important questions we have to decide!" says Mishka.

The boys give him a dirty look, but nobody says anything.

"What do you say we go get a beer?" Mishka says. "We'll all chip in. And not do any thinking!"

He gets no reply.

"This is boring!" says Mishka. "I've had enough, boys. I'm going off to do some studying."

The others stay on. We're waiting for the finale. They stand there and nothing happens. Complete absence of drama. They stand motionless for a long time, until it's almost physically unbearable, and they do nothing. No action whatsoever!

The radio is on and reporting: A hydroelectric station has gone into operation; there is fighting in Angola; Castro has made a speech. The world rushes ahead while they just stand there.

They stand. Stand. Stand!

8. A LETTER TO PETER

"Peter!" It's Chernyshev's voice, but he himself is sitting in the foreground in an army truck with some other draftees and looking silently ahead. "It's Chernyshev, Viktor, who's writing you. Remember him? Yes, that's the one. You'll be surprised that I've written you a letter. You think it's out of loneliness? I don't intend to write to anyone besides my mother and you, if you don't mind.

"There's a lot that I'd really like to talk to you about, but I decided to write you a letter. You know that I respect you and think you're a regular guy. Unfortunately, there aren't many of those in our life—I personally have met very few.

"If you feel like it, write me—I'm telling you frankly, I'd like to correspond with you.

"It will be a long time before we see one another—three years [universal military service has since been changed to two years, plus preparatory courses in high school]. You won't recognize me—no one will. I'll come back a completely different person and live in a different way. I know this for sure, and you can believe me. I am just now realizing how uninteresting and colorless my nineteen years have been. Everyone says those are the best years, and I idled them away on the street corner, so to speak.

"When I return, everything will be different. I want to study, I want to go somewhere and begin a new life.

"I want to enjoy myself and live with gusto, as they say. Not only for my sake, but so that others are pleased as well. Get me right—I am not a Philistine.

"Write me if you feel like it. I want to read an interesting book. What do you recommend?

Your friend—I hope to be one!
VIKTOR CHERNYSHEV

"P.S. Write me about what's going on in the outside world. How are things in Moscow? Again, a soldier's greeting to you! —Chernyshev, Viktor."

Moscow winter

(*Soviet Life*)

PART FIVE

Feeling for the Land and the Culture

The deeply felt attachment that Russians have for their land and its age-old ways often expresses itself in a rush of feeling, triggered by some familiar tactile experience. In Moscow it could be waking up to a dazzling sunshine after a week of gray pall that has hung persistently over the city. Or a day out in a village in late March, when the quiet frozen river begins to break up into great jagged chunks of ice that crash noisily downstream, and on that day you can already see in your mind's eye the explosion of Russian spring that will soon blanket the countryside in wildflowers. It could be watching Natalya Bessmertnova dance at the Bolshoi that triggers this feeling, but it is more apt to be something as simple as suddenly coming upon the smell of fresh dark bread. I know a woman who returned to Moscow after years abroad, and for the first few days she could not pass a bakery without going in to sniff and taste that good Russian bread. It could also be the sight of an old man's finely wrinkled face that starts you thinking about the whole country and what it has lived through. Whatever the feelings, they are intensely felt by Russians, who have a way of expressing themselves very openly.

"A FEAST OF ROWANBERRIES"

Many of Russia's older writers came out of the countryside, for the great migration to the city began when they had already reached adulthood. They understand the village as only those can who grew up there, whose "bare feet wore paths" in the fields. Some of them have produced a remarkable body of literature about the village, and as more of the young generation grows up entirely in the city, these "village" writers become a bridge to the countryside for those who have never really known it. Yet one of the best of them, Alexander Yashin, tells how difficult it is for him to communicate to his urban offspring the attachment he feels to the land and the peasants. This is part of a story of his that appeared in the magazine Soviet Literature, *No. 6, 1966.*

Spring had come to the country round Moscow and I went clambering up into the attic to put away my skis. There I noticed some clusters of dried rowanberries hanging from the rafters. I had gathered them in the autumn with my own hands, threaded them onto strings, forgotten them, and, indeed, would never have remembered had it not been for the skis.

In the old days, in the district where I was born, rowanberries were preserved for the winter just like mushrooms and other edible wild wood berries. They were also used as a cure for carbon dioxide poisoning from the fumes of a carelessly heated stove, and for headaches.

I remember once when we decided to freeze the cockroaches out of our izba [peasant hut], we opened the door and all the windows, propping them wide with wooden faggots, and moved out to the neighbors'. This was the accepted way to get rid of cockroaches in the winter in almost every household. After a few days of really hard frost not one of the armored invaders would be left, even in the deepest cracks and crannies. We returned to our izba a week later and mother's first care was to get the stove going; but she closed the flue too soon, and toward evening we were all stretched out on the damp floor like so many cockroaches ourselves. I don't know what we should have done then without our frozen rowanberries. It may seem strange, but my memory of this incident is an entirely happy one.

Here, in the Moscow district, I had really gone gathering rowanberries only because they reminded me of childhood and because they had been particularly abundant last year, and it had seemed a shame to see the thrushes pecking away at the luscious fruit.

The clusters of berries hung like birch brooms right under the roof beams of the dark attic. The leaves had dried on the twigs, crinkled up and wound round on themselves, and the hard frozen berries were also a little wrinkled, like raisins, but to make up for it had become good to eat. A fresh rowanberry is rather bitter and altogether too sharp to the taste, as difficult to eat as an unripe cranberry. But the rowanberry, like the cranberry, acquires some incomparable quality when touched with frost: there is still a hint of tartness, but, at the same time, it is sweet and leaves no bitter aftertaste.

The color of the rowanberries had also changed in the course of the winter. It had grown softer and richer in tone: from brown, almost a nut color, to amber and brilliant lemon yellow. Though why one should compare a rowanberry to a lemon, or a lemon to a rowanberry, for that matter, is more than I can say.

Having tried out the berries there and then in the attic, my first reaction was one of pleasure that I had come across a new treat for my children and yet another proof to give them that a country childhood was not only no worse but, in a great many ways, even better than a town childhood.

I do not know quite how to explain or convey this, but I am always bitterly conscious of the abyss dividing me from my children.

It is not a question of age. It is that I always was and always will be a countryman, whereas my children are town children, and the enormous city in which I am still unaccustomed to living is for them a dearly loved home. And the other thing is that I am not only a backwoodsman from the resinous depths of the pine forests; I am a peasant's son, and they have not the first idea what it means to be a peasant's son. Just try explaining to them that, even now, my whole life is geared to the life of the village where I was born. When the people from my district are finding life hard, so am I. When things are looking up for them, they look up for me, too, and I write more easily. I am profoundly concerned with everything that goes on upon that patch of mother earth where my bare feet once wore paths; in those fields that I once plowed; in the meadows where I scythed and stacked the hay.

With every pore of my skin, I feel the approach of the thaw and wait for the moment when this particular patch of earth will be free of snow. It is not a matter of indifference to me what crops are to be sown this year, what kind of harvest they will yield and whether it will be enough to provide the cattle with fodder to last them the winter, and the people with bread. I cannot help wondering from day to day whether my village has got around to building a shelter for their machines or whether these are still going to rust under the open sky, or when all the spare parts they need to keep the work going smoothly are to become available, or when the first good roads will be laid through my native district, or when the still roofless log house will become a club, or when my fellow-villagers will finally give up swigging vodka and breaking their wives' hearts because of it.

And then again: How many talented children are growing up now in my village? Will they all make their way in the world? Will somebody notice them before it is too late? And what will they do in life?

In the mornings I seem to hear the creaking of the wooden poles above the wells in our village street and the tinkling of the cold, transparent water as it pours out of the wooden dipper into the zinc buckets. Are the well-poles still creaking? Is the well just near our izba still there, the one from which, for so many years, I fetched the water in two yoked buckets?

What is all that to my sons and daughters? At any rate, they are not peasant's children and, or so it always seems to me, for this very reason have no feeling or understanding for my childhood. We are different kinds of people, not cut from the same cloth, and therefore, I suppose, we have different ways of looking at the world, at the earth and at the sky. But perhaps I am not right, it's almost impossible to tell! I am tormented by jealousy and a feeling of injury whenever the curtain descends between us, when my know-it-all offspring take it into their heads to rebel and to tease me because, with every summer, I feel the pull not of the warm lands and the blue sea, but of my northern wilderness with all its gnats and mosquitoes. They detest gnats and mosquitoes. And who can blame them? It is not everyone who enjoys the company of such evil emanations of our planet.

The reek of cowshed and stable, of freshly manured fields and of straw affects me as a stimulant and reminds me of freshly baked bread, whereas for my children the smell of manure is nothing but a stink.

The artist Serov has a wonderful picture called "Oxen"—
the old Serov, that is, not the present one. I cannot really
believe my children capable of appreciating the full charm
of this masterpiece. Even when my sons do get out into the
country, they are more interested in a tractor than in a live
horse, the most perfect creature formed by nature. It is
easier to manage a machine than a living being.

True, even country children nowadays prefer to play at
tractors and cars, rather than at horses, just as during the
war they all played soldier. Perhaps my fears are exaggerated.
Nevertheless, I still occasionally feel sorry for my children.

Sorry for them because, as town children, they have less
contact with the country than I should wish. I think they
must lose something because of this, something indefinable
but wholesome, which simply passes them by. It seems to me
that to live close to nature and to work lovingly to assist her
in her labors and transformations makes a man more simple,
gentle, and kind. I know of no other place of work for ennobling man and giving him peace of mind.

One way and another, I am sorry for my children; but I
love them and therefore lose no opportunity to stand up for
my country pedigree, my fathers and my forefathers.

And now, having come across these rowanberries that I had
forgotten in the attic and remembered how much we had
enjoyed eating them frozen when we were children, I thought
to myself with renewed hope: Now I shall make a feast for
them, and my fledglings will catch the feeling of the real
country and the real Russia, and we shall understand one
another better.

A WALK IN

DOSTOYEVSKY'S CITY

*In Leningrad you still get a wonderfully imme-
diate sense of the Russian nineteenth century—
the elegant homes of St. Petersburg and the old
quarters of the working class, the palaces of the
Tsars, and the museums and parks and broad
squares of the city. You have a sense of events in
history that actually happened and those in literature that you feel must have happened, because they are so vivid to people the world over.
Even small events, such as Anna Karenina's going
to the opera house on the night Adelina Patti
sang—a joining of literature and life that seems
natural in this city. There is Pushkin's Petersburg,
and Lermontov's, and Turgenyev's, and, of
course, Dostoyevsky's. Here, a contemporary
writer, Daniil Granin, describes an unusual walking tour he made under the guidance of Dostoyevsky's grandson, who died before the material came out in the magazine* Soviet Literature, *No. 8, 1968, as part of a larger travelogue.*

Once, together with Dostoyevsky's grandson, Andrei
Fyodorovich Dostoyevsky, I made a tour of the places connected with the novel *Crime and Punishment.* We were accompanied by a friend of mine, the Czech scholar and specialist on Dostoyevsky František Kautmann. The walk was

originally undertaken for his benefit. I am a Leningrader through and through. I love Dostoyevsky and, naturally, I thought I knew everything; if I didn't happen to know this or that address, it was of no particular importance, because such details were necessary, if at all, only to the research worker. So we set out under the guidance of Andrei Fyodorovich, a most remarkable man, incidentally, in his own right. An engineer, a war veteran, when he went on pension he dedicated himself entirely to the affairs of his renowned grandfather. The first time I met him, he was busy with the arrangements for organizing a Dostoyevsky museum in the writer's Leningrad apartment, and since then I had had more than one opportunity to convince myself of his very thorough knowledge of the smallest details bound up with Dostoyevsky's life in Petersburg. And now, as we came out into the Maiorov Prospekt, Andrei Fyodorovich began to tell us what had stood where in those years, a hundred years ago, that is —the gambling houses, taverns, and pubs here and on the neighboring streets. He saw the area with the eyes of Dostoyevsky's contemporaries, knowing in detail the history of every house. It was extremely interesting to listen to him, as it is to listen to any historian on his special subject, until the moment when he said, pointing to one of the houses: "Those were the gates, and there was a stone in the courtyard under which Raskolnikov hid the valuables he had taken from the old woman." His words carried complete conviction and, seeing the surprise on our faces, he opened the novel *Crime and Punishment* at a marked page and read out:

"Coming out of V Prospekt toward the square, he saw on the left a passage leading between two blank walls to a courtyard. On the right hand, the blank unwhitewashed wall of a four-story house stretched far into the court."

And further on there was a detailed description of that far place where lay a big, unhewn stone.

The house had been rebuilt, but Andrei Fyodorovich had

looked up the old plans, and, according to them, everything corresponded exactly. Even so, I must admit, I was not convinced; I thought it was a coincidence, a matter of chance, no more.

We turned off to the right from Przhevalsky Street, and Andrei Fyodorovich led us to house No. 19, informing us that it was the home of Raskolnikov. The house and the courtyard were in an appalling state. There was mud in the courtyard, rubbish bins were tipped over on one side, there were rags and some old broken chairs. We walked up the worn stone steps to the narrow, dark staircase with the semicircular stairwell to Raskolnikov's garret:

"His garret was under the roof of a high five-story house. The landlady who provided him with garret, dinners, and attendance lived on the floor below, and every time he went out he was obliged to pass her kitchen, the window of which invariably stood open."

There was a garret with thirteen steps leading up to it, just as it said in the novel, and there was a staircase past this apartment with its kitchen, and the kitchen window itself gave straight onto the landing.

But perhaps the other staircases in this house were planned the same way? No, of all the staircases this was the only one that corresponded to the description, and nowhere else was there a kitchen with a window. But, assuming this to be true, is it of any significance to the novel, is it worth taking into consideration? That, however, was the whole point: The geography of the locale had great importance, in the first place, for Raskolnikov himself. His actions were conditioned by this kitchen, it was here that he saw the ax he needed to commit his murder. But coming out onto the staircase, he saw that Nastya was in the kitchen and that therefore he could not take the ax. Suddenly, those "details" he had always despised and considered unimportant in comparison with his own will power and his main ideas began to work against him; they suddenly came to life and defeated his intention.

Andrei Fyodorovich read, and we followed all of Raskolnikov's movements, went down into the courtyard, under the gates where Raskolnikov had stood aimlessly, humiliated and crushed, until at last he saw another ax in the porter's lodge. And the porter's lodge had two steps down to it (two—no more and no less). We glanced into the damp darkness, it was now a neglected storeroom. Then we emerged and continued on our way to the house of the old woman, the pawnbroker.

"He had not far to go; he knew indeed how many steps it was from the gates of his lodging house: exactly seven hundred and thirty."

With gradually increasing empathy for Raskolnikov, we also counted our steps, and, with a kind of fear clutching at our hearts, approached "a huge house which on one side looked onto the canal, and on the other side onto the street." The house had happily retained the same appearance and was painted a hideous dirty pink. "There was a continual coming and going through the two gates and in the two courtyards of the house." In the courtyard a multitude of unpleasing windows followed our every movement from either side. Along the narrow, dark stairway, where the well-rubbed brass knobs were still in evidence on the banisters, we went up to the fourth floor to the old woman's apartment and halted before the door. On the stairs we met no one. By now we were identifying ourselves completely with Raskolnikov; even our hands were trembling. I had no more doubts. And later, when Andrei Fyodorovich took us to the police station, the precise location of which he had also determined by consulting old records, this also corresponded convincingly to the description in the novel: a new house, gates, to the right the staircase, narrow, steep. And not far away the house where the Marmeladovs lived—Kozel's house. And the haberdashery store, and the tavern.

Along the street with its rough cobbles strolled a skinny little old woman with a dog on a leash. The old woman was wearing a black lace cape and the dog a nylon vest. At the corner some old men were playing chess on a crate. Two drunks approached them and, doffing their straw hats, asked: "What's your attitude toward ex-jailbirds?"

The water in the Griboyedov Canal was greenish, dirty-looking. On the Sennaya Square, or Peace Square, as it is now, near the old guardhouse where Dostoyevsky had been imprisoned, a heavily painted woman was walking. She looked at us with the eyes of Sonechka. Nonsense, I said to myself, absolute nonsense, it's just that we're in that sort of mood and we're seeing things accordingly.

It was something else, though, something quite different that was giving me no peace, something of much graver importance: Why had Dostoyevsky had to be so accurate? After all, there never had been a real Raskolnikov. But his garret, the thirteen steps leading up to it? There they were to this day. So that meant that Dostoyevsky himself must have been in all these places and chosen this particular staircase and this particular garret for the habitation of his hero, and then chosen the house and the apartment of the old woman. That he himself had sought out and walked all the way Raskolnikov was to go, and more than once, for he had counted the steps and the stairs. Therefore, he must have reenacted the scene for himself in full, and the other scenes, with the precision of a police report, he had acted like a detective. No, not even like a detective, for the policeman follows up a crime that has already been committed, and Dostoyevsky was the first to commit the crime in the image of Raskolnikov—more than that, he had first to plan out the whole topography, to find suitable accommodation for his hero. But why, the question arises, why did he need to be so accurate, all those exact addresses; could he not imagine, think up a garret with an imaginary staircase, create the details, create the house and flat of the old woman? Surely it would have been both quicker and easier. Neither Andrei Fyodorovich nor František could give me an answer.

There is a somewhat similar feeling about Dickens. An underlying exactitude of description suggesting the existence of real addresses.

In those minutes when we had stood in the gateway before the porter's lodge where Raskolnikov had seen the ax shining at him from under the bench, when we had read how Raskolnikov, crushed and humiliated by his bad luck until that moment, had taken a new lease on life, pounced on the ax, dragged it out from under the bench, and concealed it beneath his coat, attaching it by the loop, I observed that this particular incident we were seeing and experiencing had made a particularly strong impression on František. The element of chance seemed strange to him, pregnant with significance. I did not immediately grasp wherein lay the difference in our understanding of this incident: it only became clear to me in London. For František the ax was not an object of everyday use, common, quite indispensable to the town life of that time. Indeed, not only of that time. For me it was perfectly natural that the porter should have had an ax. Until quite recently, the majority of Leningrad houses were heated by tiled Russian stoves. Stacks of wood were piled high in every courtyard. Since childhood I had been accustomed to sawing wood, to chopping logs, to carrying them home in bundles. There was an ax in every apartment and, it went without saying, in every porter's lodge. And though František had lived and studied in Moscow and has a good knowledge of the way we live, one cannot expect him to react to the ax as a Russian would react. Yes, it is only now that I have, I think, begun to understand something of what is hidden behind such superficially obvious popular conceptions as Dostoyevsky's Petersburg or Dickens's London.

A SMALL CULTURAL

OUTPOST IN SIBERIA

From Dostoyevsky's Petersburg it is a long way to a village in Siberia where a twelve-year-old girl, arrested and exiled with her family during the World War II years, found inspiration to develop a great love for literature. The following is from The Endless Steppe: Growing Up in Siberia, *by Esther Hautzig.*

There was one place where I forgot the cold—indeed, forgot Siberia. That was in the library. There, in that muddy village, was a great institution. Not physically, to be sure, but in every other way imaginable. It was a small log cabin, immaculately attended to with loving care; it was well lighted with oil lamps and it was *warm.* But best of all, it contained a small but amazing collection from the world's best literature, truly amazing considering the time, the place, and its size. From floor to ceiling it was lined with books—books, books, books. It was there that I was to become acquainted with the works of Dumas, Pasternak's translations of Shakespeare, the novels of Mark Twain, Jack London, and, of course, the Russians. It was in that log cabin that I escaped from Siberia—either reading there or taking the books home. It was between that library and two extraordinary teachers that I developed a lifelong passion for the great Russian novelists and poets.

ALONG THE ROAD

Yuri Kazakov's short stories are a revelation of people's moods and outlooks and the impulses that make them behave as they do. He has such a fine sense of earth's nature and its moods as well that you can practically smell the country-side where his people live. "Along the Road" is one of my favorite Kazakovs. It is reprinted from Going to Town and Other Stories, Yuri Kazakov, *compiled and translated by Gabriella Azrael, Houghton Mifflin Company, Boston, 1964. You can learn more about Russian life from a story such as this one—by reading it slowly and letting yourself enter in, with an eye on the wonderful detail of it—than you can learn from a dozen articles that consciously set out to explain how things really are. It would be hard to convey more effectively why it is that, in spite of the hardship of life there, the great wilderness of Siberia keeps drawing young people out to explore it and to take part in the taming of small segments of it.*

1

The end of winter came as usual. The snow suddenly disappeared, leaving the ground smoking and steaming in the sun. The stallions kicked at the sides of their stalls and gnawed at the grooms' hands. Then the bulls began bellowing, shaking the oaken beams of the barn where they had been chained for the winter. The thrushes did stunts at the edge of the forest, the starlings whistled at sundown, the cherry trees in the ravine began to blossom drunkenly. The countryside, stripped shamelessly naked by winter, secretly began to cover itself with berries, birches, and lilacs.

And the fields were already a misty green, and the road was already awash, the dry summer was already on its way when Ilya Snegirev packed up again for Siberia.

He had decided to go in February.

One night, worn out from driving all day, Ilya had come out of the office of the tree farm and crossed the forest clearing covered with fallen branches, going toward his truck. His truck—like his jacket, his boots, his hands, and his hat— smelled of gas. But Snegirev was aware of no odors, except the smell of dust in the summer and frost in the winter.

That particular February night the thaw had begun. Above him the sky was turning green, above the forest it was glowing darkly; the trees were black and swollen. Spring was clearly in the air. Ilya smelled, listened, blew his nose, and, getting into the cab, made up his mind.

It was not the first time spring had torn him away. Last year he'd been in Siberia—suffered through a whole summer there—and had returned in the fall deeply disappointed. He didn't like barracks life and he loathed Siberia, with its vile taiga, and the distant noise of trucks straining along the roads.

When Snegirev had returned that fall the ground was streaked with blackish snow. The woods were naked and dead. The grass hummed and trembled in the wind, and the first dustings of snow melted overnight. But then the real snow fell, to freeze and thaw, and Snegirev settled happily back to work.

His job kept him driving night and day—to the station, to the woods, to neighboring regions. He'd stop for the night anywhere, getting up at dawn to heat water, fill the radiator, and start the motor. Then he'd have a quick glass of tea and exchange a few words with his host, all the while enjoying the roar of the engine in the street.

He loved driving the lonely roads at night, when it seems you're the only one in the world who isn't sleeping, and the truck wavers and drowses, and the blinding spot of the headlight leaps ahead toward the horizon.

Alone at night, thinking idly about the past, he began to forget his grudge against Siberia; the bad part grew so dim it was as if it had never been, and all that remained were the power and beauty of the mountains, of the raging, un-Russian rivers, of the heavy concrete contours of the dams.

So, having decided to go there again, Snegirev began to settle his affairs a week before his departure in May.

2

He wakes every morning in a holiday mood. Nights, he dresses up and goes around saying goodbye to his neighbors. He has the quiet air of someone celebrating something special, but gradually, he begins to talk about Siberia. He talks long and well, and his friends' faces begin to cloud with envy; they'd also like to see Siberia.

Ilya gets home late every night, taking off his shoes and walking around in his stocking feet, thinking his mother asleep. The last evening he spends at home packing, having said all his goodbyes during the week. For the first time he notices the sadness in his mother's face, her tearful eyes. In bed, thinking about Siberia and about leaving his mother alone, he is alternately happy and sad. He smokes furtively and just can't get to sleep.

Ilya leaves the next morning, not especially early. No one is seeing him off but his mother, because he doesn't like to be seen off. His mother has been crying all morning, and now, walking along with her son, she sighs but keeps up a conversation about this and that.

Leaving the farm, where the road turns sharply to the right past the thicket, they run into the truck bringing a load of bricks from the station. Mishka Firsov, Ilya's friend and neighbor, has taken Ilya's place at the wheel.

The Snegirevs step to the side. Covering them with a light coat of spring dust, Mishka calls something to them. Putting on the brake, he jumps out and comes back.

"You mean you're really going?" he asks, shaking hands. Mishka smells of gasoline now.

"I'm going," says Ilya.

"Look here, maybe you won't like it this time either."

"I'll like it all right," Ilya mutters tensely. He's listening to his mother starting to breathe unevenly.

"Ech, I guess we've had our fun, the two of us," says Mishka, looking at the truck. The motor is still running. "Here, have a last cigarette."

They smoke for a while without saying anything.

"And what about Tamara?" Mishka remembers. "Is that all over?"

"What about her?" Ilya answers indifferently. "If she wants to, she'll come."

"Oh. Well, let's shake on it, then!"

"Right."

They'd like to embrace but are too embarrassed. They simply shake hands.

"Going straight to the train?" asks Mishka.

"We'll just about make it," says Ilya, shifting impatiently.

"And I've got to be back at the station in half an hour. Well, *gud bai!*"

Mishka hurries into the truck, and Ilya and his mother go on. A minute later they hear Mishka stepping heavily on the gas.

Summer in the countryside   (*Soviet Life*)

His mother doesn't say anything for a long time, shielding her eyes from the sun with her scarf. Finally she says, absently, "I tell you, Tamara is *perfection* next to your other girls." She pronounces "perfection" with great care and is evidently satisfied with the result. "Yes, and she really loves you, too, not like all those flirts."

Ilya doesn't say anything, but his mother needs to talk. So she speaks of Tamara, of how they'll put a new roof on the house this summer, of when it will be her turn to tend the farm's kitchen garden, and again of Tamara. Ilya takes a look at his watch and quickens his step. His mother hurries and stumbles. Her thoughts are confused.

"Well, son—" she says and stops.

Ilya also stops, looks at the fading, myopic, loving eyes of his mother, and begins to scratch his nose. His mouth is drooping, he feels numb all over, but he thrusts out his chin, and cocks his eyebrows, assuming a casual expression.

"Let me— you—" his mother murmurs, making the sign of the cross. "Go on now, go on, you've got to go. I— I'll follow for a little bit."

"I'll write you, Mama," Ilya says in a thin voice, kissing her awkwardly. Don't get sick."

"Don't you stay too long, and dress warmly. Maybe it's still cold there in Siberia," his mother says, trying not to cry.

"Now stop this, Mama," Ilya answers, too cheerfully. "Is this the first time I've gone away or something? You take care, write me everything. And I'll send money as soon as I get some."

He hugs her again and turns and walks quickly down the road. He snuffles, his eyes sting, and his throat is full. He relaxes after a few hundred feet and begins to breathe more easily. The bridge of his nose is no longer throbbing, and his face takes on the same look of intense concentration it has had all week.

He looks up at the lacy clouds, the muscles in his face move, and he swallows, already seeing the river, flowing through Yeniseisk, the rocky hills, and the taiga, and the pale electric lights of the towns at work on a white night.

Another hundred feet and he looks around. His mother is still following him, shielding her face with her hand. Ilya stops, takes out his handkerchief and waves. His mother doesn't respond.

Doesn't see me, he thinks in disappointment. Sighing, he goes on.

And just as he is beginning to walk faster, and with more

determination, his mother stops and waves to him with a radiant smile. It seems to her that her son has turned and is looking at her. She can even make out his features. She's amazed how well she can see through her tears.

Far off in the fields, a spot is moving on the horizon—a girl is running along the edge of the forest. That's how my mother ran once, he thinks sadly and tenderly. When he looks back, his mother is so far behind that he can't tell whether she has stopped or is still following.

She is, she can't make herself turn back. Tears are running down her face, and she wipes them away with the ends of her scarf. She has no need to hold herself in any more, alone there on the road. Oh God, she thinks. No use for their own homes. On the go. Always on the go. The country's all torn up these days. He used to run around in just a shirt and his little bare feet, holy mother of God! And now he's gone, flown away.

She stops, sobs, and raises her hand to her eyes. Ilya has been out of sight a long time, dissolved in the azure horizon, but it seems to his mother that she can see him. He has turned and is waving goodbye. She takes a deep fluttery breath and limply waves in answer.

A WORKING SUMMER

ON THE

ISLANDS UP NORTH

Some university students and young intellectuals spend their vacations helping to restore Russia's churches and monasteries that have fallen into decay. There is an air of urgency about their work, a feeling that time is running out. They must salvage what is left after years of hostility by the Communist Party toward the Russian religious past—an attitude that was widely interpreted at the grass-roots level as a sanction for acts of scorn and vandalism. Churches became storehouses for grain and potatoes, and hundreds of very old ones were destroyed by fire. Now the Party has come around to a more civilized outlook, which means that funds are available for some restoration work. The young people who take part in this work find satisfaction at several different levels, as you will see in these excerpts from the diary of a young man who led a group to the Solovetsky Islands in the White Sea. His diary appeared in the magazine Soviet Life *in January, 1968.*

June 25

Solovetsky! How much that word says to all of us. To the old people it speaks of chiming bells and the lonely melancholy of one of the most venerable and biggest monasteries in old Russia. To us the islands are history, but our history. We want to understand the history of our people, to know ourselves and make connection with our native land, a country that has been on the scene for hundreds of years.

And so ninety of us, mostly Moscow University undergraduates, are going to the Solovetsky Islands to help restore the monastery and build roads and bridges. We are going for one month. We will not be paid, except for transportation and meals, but we are going anyway.

June 30
We're off!
This will be my seventh trip to the White Sea. That is probably why I was chosen to head the team, which has a

University students at work in the Solovetsky Islands   (*Novosti*)

very important-sounding title: the Solovetsky Restoration
and Building Detachment of Moscow University.

We fill two railroad cars. I don't see many people I know,
even though most of them are from the physics department.
There are fifteen math students and a few historians and
philologists. There is even an actor, also an undergraduate.
Almost all of them are upperclassmen—and with experience;
they worked on the Virgin Land development project in Kazakhstan. These are people who can work with their hands as
well as their heads.

The last two days before we left were crammed with telephone calls. "Take me with you. I'm willing to do any kind
of work!" Mostly girls. I told them it would be hard work;
this is the North, after all. But they begged and begged, and I
had to give in. So now almost half the group consists of girls.

July 3

It takes a lot to make a Muscovite sit up, especially a college student. But when our ship, the *Bukovina*, approached
the islands toward evening, the students who lined the rail-
ing gaped. From out of the gray mist, as though out of a
legend, rose the famous Solovetsky Kremlin.

The delicate pastel colors of the northern sky are unrivaled,
and so is the beauty of the odd-shaped lakes and the winding
canals the monks built. There are more than 400 lakes on the
islands, filled with fish. Muskrat breed here. It all seems like
a miracle when you remember that the Arctic Circle is only
100 miles away.

July 5

We live in the monastery, in the refectory where the
monks used to feed pilgrims. Pilgrims came from as far away
as the Volga, the Urals, Karelia and the Don.

Actually, what our restoration amounts to, so far, is clearing the monastery of debris. We're carrying out refuse piled up there for centuries.

The local people gave us a hospitable enough welcome but seem doubtful about our abilities. The authorities are not at all sure that Moscow intellectuals know what work means. The fishermen and the workers stare at us curiously, as though they have their doubts, too.

July 8

The weather is sunny, even hot. So are the nights, the famous "white nights." We stroll around practically all night. In groups and also in pairs. And come to work sleepy but cheerful.

I've been wondering why there are so many physics students in our group. Why is it that Moscow University physics students were the first ones to volunteer to build houses, hospitals and barns in the Virgin Lands of Kazakhstan? And the same here. Although we're not really building here; we're restoring historical and architectural monuments. This is a cultural virgin land.

I think it is because physicists and mathematicians, even while they are undergraduates, deal so much with scientific abstractions. They may not see the results of their work for years—not within a reasonable future. And people need to see results more immediately. And so you have physicists and mathematicians spending their vacations doing manual work all over the country.

Here on the islands they are getting obvious pleasure out of building the wooden sidewalks traditional in the North and fixing the roads.

July 17

We can feel the attitude of the local people changing. They see that we keep at it. They have been inviting us to their homes for a glass of milk and a talk. The people here are reticent but kind, even sentimental.

July 20

Thousands of tourists come to the islands. Many are disappointed when they see how this once flourishing area has declined.

Now the Solovetsky Islands have been declared a national preserve. But it needs people to save this monument of Russian history for future generations. The islands make one think. They have torn us away from the automated routine of city life and its superficial judgments.

"OLD RUSSIA HAS
BECOME FASHIONABLE"

*How did it start and what does it mean, this
preoccupation with Old Russia that finds expression in so many ways? Not just in the restoration
of churches, but in the icons that once hung inside them and now hang in Moscow apartments,
in movies and a wealth of books on the cultural
past, in exhibits of old folk art and handicrafts,
and in articles of clothing such as the huge flow-
ered shawls with the fringe that were coveted by
some of Moscow's elite theater-going women
back around 1966. To Yefim Dorosh, who is well
versed in cultural Russia, there is food for
thought in all this, and he shares some of his reflections in the first and last parts of a book
review that was published in the magazine* Novy
mir *[New World], No. 3, 1969.*

In 1958 or 1959—I no longer remember exactly—I
was walking around the Rostov Kremlin one early September
evening. It was still light out, and the clear sky over the city
had turned pink from the setting sun, while inside the Kremlin between the palaces and churches whose brick walls give
off a dampness, the twilight had fallen.

Usually at this hour, when the museum is already closed,
there is no one here, and I was startled by the loud voices of

people calling to one another as if they were excited about something, and then by the people themselves, who, by all appearances, were not from the local area, being dressed the way people in Moscow are. Craning their necks, pausing from time to time, hurrying one another along, and, it seemed, unable to tear themselves away from the spectacle of those white churches soaring into the sky with golden crosses on their cupolas, they dashed from one spot to another.

Two or three of them hailed me and asked, "What is this place?"

Then the others gathered around—about fifteen of them— and began to inquire, "What is this, when was it built?" When I replied that this was the Rostov Kremlin, they were all extremely surprised: Why the Rostov one?

I began to tell about the builder of the Kremlin, Ion Sysoyevich, and about his highly placed patron, the Patriarch Nikon. All at once I realized that my listeners, who, it turned out, were Moscow actors on tour in the Yaroslavl region, not only had never heard anything about the famous Rostov Metropolitan, but had only a dim notion of when—in what period—Nikon lived. As for the existence of still another Rostov besides the one on the Don River, this was quite a discovery for them.

I told them that the city they were now in would be 1,100 years old in another three years, and this amazed them—that it was even older than Moscow. Moreover, it seemed to me they didn't understand just how old this was, and it was only when I explained that Rostov was mentioned in the chronicles under the same year as the mission of the Varangians that the breath of time somehow touched each one of them, and they all became respectfully quiet. They knew about the legendary Rurik, even if only from hearsay.

They dashed to their waiting bus, and I suddenly realized what an extraordinary sensation these people had just had. After Zagorsk, which they knew as a place where foreigners

Old Russia: village and birch trees   (*Soviet Life*)

go and where people study for the priesthood; after Pereslavl-Zalesski, whose old monuments are dispersed among the provincial houses and which is known to Muscovites mainly for a lake where many people go fishing; after the fir forests in the midst of which a highway runs over the hills; and after the provincial town of Petrovsk, which is charming but hardly surprising to anybody—after all this, on a clear and quiet evening at the end of September, they saw rising above the lake toward the violet twilight sky the many white towers and the many cupolas of Rostov, brilliant with silver leaf and shining with gold.

It was as if something had fallen, and in the yawning gap

that was left, clearly discernable from afar, through the many centuries, there appeared—not the forgotten—simply the unknown, and therefore unremembered, Ancient Russia.

Since then, ten years have passed.

Old Russia has become fashionable, and as with any fashion there is a lot here that is naive and amusing and even banal. Nearly every day you can find in some newspaper or magazine an article or sketch on the subject of Russian antiquities or folk art. In itself this is cause for joy, but the excessive use of such epithets as "fantastic" and of the words "fairytale" and "legend"—one writer called Rublyev's wooden church a "wooden tale"—gives many of these writings a touch of saccharine.

Yet this fashion, like the foam on the surface that reveals things going on deep down in the water, is a sign of certain profound social processes.

Once in Kirillov, by the cafeteria (called a cafe in the evening), where in summertime you almost always meet someone you know from Moscow or Leningrad, I noticed a bearded boy and a girl in glasses, both in green hiking clothes and both bent under their huge knapsacks, asking a militiaman where the road to Belozersk was.

The militiaman started to explain how to get to the bus station when the boy retorted that it wasn't a bus they needed, but the road, because they were going on foot. The militiaman said it was forty kilometers to Belozersk, to which the girl replied that they had already walked two hundred kilometers, and she added somewhat mischievously that if he felt sorry for them, he could give them money for bus tickets.

Then, looking at the sign above the cafeteria and checking their watches, the young people began to whisper to one another. They must have decided they couldn't afford to eat in the cafe, for they went off in the direction of Belozersk, swaying under the weight of their knapsacks.

"In dividing up the cities among his men, he gave Polotesk to one, Rostov to another, and Belo-ozero to a third"—those words came back to me, and I thought how ancient the history of Russia has become in our day, how its origins have receded into the depths of centuries—if not in the chronicles, then in the living memories of the people who are traveling along the roads of the country, which bears the imprint in many of its details of the affairs and traditions of centuries long past.

Precisely in the details, because it is from this kind of a trip that the memory brings back pictures of the natural surroundings our ancestors lived in, of the appearance of the buildings inside and outside, with a fully tangible sense of the stone and wood from which they are built. The memory brings back the subjects of the old wall paintings, which make it possible to judge not only what themes were widespread but also about the favorite designs of woven fabric, about the working tools that were customarily used at that time, and, finally, about the peculiarities of speech and the characteristic words and expressions going back almost to those times when "the Slavs came from the Danube and settled near Lake Ilmen, and others settled along the Desna River and along the Sena and Sula Rivers, and that is how the Slav language spread."

One day, when I was writing these notes, I happened to see a painting by V. Popkov called *Northern Song*, at a Moscow exhibition. The painting showed young townspeople, students or scientists, most likely, gathered in a peasant house and listening to elderly women singing, probably at their request.

This would seem to be a genre scene, and not such a rare one in our time, when the summer brings young people with knapsacks to the old northern towns and villages—girls like that one in the corner, leaning on her elbows on the table and gazing pensively out the window, where one can see a deep, quiet river illumined by the rays of the setting sun; or that bearded youth who has turned away from the singing women and is staring, also pensively, out another window; or those boys who are practically children, the one wearing glasses, holding his hand against his cheek and sitting absolutely still on a bench opposite the singers, and the other next to him, in sneakers and a loose sweater, with fine features and curly hair falling low on his forehead and the back of his neck.

I won't discuss the artistic merits of the painting—a very talented one, I thought. Like every important work of art, it evoked thoughts and feelings that went far beyond the framework of the real event the artist had depicted.

Perhaps the artist was not even thinking what I was thinking as I stood in front of his picture. But even if his thoughts had nothing in common with mine, even if he merely painted the widows of Mezensk, as the women are called in the title of the picture—even then, those peasant widows who more than twenty years after victory are singing, "Oh, all our husbands have been taken away to the war," bring to mind all the widows that ever were since the early morning when Yaroslavna wept by the wall in Putivl. And the way the young people are listening to them makes us feel that this is a picture of a meeting with Russia, with the history of Russia, which has been especially well preserved in the art of the North.

THE TRADITIONS OF

PEASANT WEDDINGS

The old Russian peasant wedding must have been quite an event to behold. A whole series of events, actually, that kept the village engrossed and entertained for days. Perhaps the next best thing is to read a detailed description of one; for here, all bound up in the ritual, are some of the attitudes and religious beliefs and superstitions of the peasantry. It is interesting to see how much of this ritual was still being practiced in the late 1950's, when the material for this study was gathered in Kalinin Province, a little to the northwest of Moscow. It was published in the magazine Sovetskaya etnografia [Soviet Ethnography], *No. 3, 1959.*

The wedding ritual before the Revolution consisted of three main cycles: prewedding, the actual wedding, and postwedding. The first cycle included the matchmaking, the inspection of the bridegroom's house, the closing of the deal between the two fathers by handshaking, worship, a girl's party for the bride's friends, and a stag party for the bridegroom's friends, and the ritual bathing of the bride and bridegroom in a bathhouse or in front of the stove before the wedding ceremony. The actual wedding consisted of the gathering of the wedding procession, the arrival of the bridegroom to call for the bride, the marriage ceremony, the young couple's visit to the parental homes, the delivery of the dowry, some procedures after the first wedding night, and many other rites. The wedding feast was the center of the wedding cycle. The postwedding cycle consisted of a series of parties given for the young couple by all the relatives.

Of the prewedding cycle, the matchmaking still goes on in many villages, although it has changed completely in nature. Formerly, matchmaking was reconnaissance by the relatives of the bride and the bridegroom. Often the bridegroom sent matchmakers to several girls at the same time before he made up his mind, and the bride's side also looked around for the best possible match. The question of the dowry was very important in the choice of a bride. If the matchmaking was successful, the bride's parents gave the bridegroom a "deposit" (something of value, such as a fur coat, boots, or a shawl), which the bridegroom was not expected to return if the marriage agreement was broken. The deposit custom is no longer observed, and the matchmaking now takes place only after the young couple have themselves decided to get married. The bridegroom goes to his bride's house to arrange the match himself, accompanied by his parents. The various problems connected with the wedding (date, number of guests from each side, and so forth) are discussed at the matchmaking. One topic of discussion still is what the bride will bring to the family she is entering. Formerly a dowry included a considerable sum of money in addition to clothing, linen, and bedding. The parents of the bride also expected something in exchange for their daughter; they would ask for a threshing barn, a stable, a horse, a calf, and so on—that is to say, the proceeds from the sale of these things.

Today, the bride's dowry is made up mainly of her own clothes (overcoats, dresses, lingerie) and bed linen. In recent years it is also sure to include such things as a chest of drawers, a sewing machine, a bicycle, or the like. In some places the window curtains, tablecloths, towels, and other household articles from the bride's dowry are taken to the bridegroom's house the day before the ceremony. It is still customary for the wife to bring some articles of value to her husband's family, the dowry is exhibited for all to see, and anyone who wishes may enter the house to inspect it. The young couple and, even more so, the parents are very concerned about the opinion of their fellow villagers in this matter, and they strive to do everything "as well as anyone else," so that "people will not disapprove."

The custom of "inspection of the bridegroom's house" by the bride and her parents has been preserved in some villages. In the old days, the inspection was very thorough. Often the bridegroom's parents would rent grain from neighbors and fill the bin with it or drive somebody else's cattle into their own yard in an effort to show how rich they were. Now the inspection is purely formal.

The "worship," "handshaking," and "drinking" used to take place in the bride's home a few days after the matchmaking was completed. The "worship" was attended by the bride's and the bridegroom's closest relatives, who, after making the final arrangements for the wedding, all knelt down before the icons and prayed.

After the "worship," the bride did not go out of the house until the wedding. She stayed home, sewing things for her dowry in the company of her girl friends. This sewing time was a special kind of gathering at which the girls sang wedding songs. The bridegroom would visit the bride during this period and bring gifts. Formerly, this custom of short visits helped the young couple, who often hardly knew one another, to get acquainted. Nowadays the wedding is preceded by a more or less lengthy period of friendship between the young people, and the visits are unnecessary.

Among other rituals that have disappeared are the "morning wailing" and the girls' party. In the old days, after the match was arranged, the bride would have to weep and wail every morning, thereby taking leave of her girlhood. Before the girls' party (sometimes after it) the bathing-of-the-bride ritual took place. She would go to a neighbor's house for the bathing, and the house had to be on the same side of the block, because she was forbidden to cross the street. In the peasants' view, this ensured her a good married life. The water for the bath was brought by the bride's girl friends, who drew it from different wells. There was also a ritual bathing of the bridegroom, and the bride was supposed to use a bundle of twigs given her by the bridegroom, and he was to use a similar bundle that he had received from her.

The day before the wedding, the bride gave a party for the girls and the bridegroom gave one for the young men. The girls brought a decorated fir tree (in some places, a birch tree), symbolizing virginity, into the bride's house. She said farewell to her "beautiful beauty" [virginity] and presented the ribbons from her braids to her sisters and close friends. The girls sang wedding songs.

In the past these parties symbolized a farewell to freedom and a carefree youth. Life changed a great deal after marriage, especially for the girl, who entered someone else's household. Nowadays there are no significant differences, moral or otherwise, in the way of life before and after marriage. This is apparently why these customs have disappeared from the present-day wedding ritual.

However, the decorated fir or birch tree has survived from the girls' party, and in Vesyegonsk and Sandovo districts it is the custom to nail decorated trees to the houses of the betrothed pair right after the matchmaking.

The actual wedding celebration (the banquet) has proved the longest-lasting custom and has as much importance as before. The marriage is not considered complete until the celebration has taken place. That is why an effort is made to have the civil registration of the marriage and the wedding banquet on the same day.

A lot of wine and urban-style hors d'oeuvres are served, but so are the many traditional wedding foods: meat jelly, homemade cheeses, boiled meat, porridge, omelets, butter cookies made with eggs, a pie filled with cottage cheese and decorated with flowers, gelatin dishes and *bliny*, and other kinds of pancakes. Homemade beer is also served at weddings.

In a wedding we observed on the Voroshilov Collective Farm in Vesyegonsk District, the bridegroom called for the bride in the collective farm car to take her to the village Soviet to register the marriage. When he entered the house he "purchased" a seat at the table next to the bride. He and his companions were offered wine, and a group of elderly women sang old wedding songs, standing beside the stove as is the tradition. Then the bride's mother gave her daughter her blessing and the young couple started out for the car. The path from the house to the car was covered with strips of carpet. Meanwhile, some of the young people removed the fir tree that had been nailed to the corner of the bride's house since the matchmaking. It is interesting that the old custom of decorating the wedding cavalcade has been preserved, with the girls adorning the car or the horse that is to carry the bride and groom with varicolored streamers of paper flowers (fresh flowers in summer) and embroidered towels. At the wedding we observed, the car was decorated in this manner.

The car had to stop frequently because of obstructions (logs and rocks) put in its way by men and boys. The bridegroom would offer them wine, brought along in the car for the purpose, after which the logs were cleared away. From the registry office the young couple drove through their own and all the surrounding villages "so that everybody could see how the Voroshilov Collective Farm celebrates a wedding."

Shortly after the pair had left for the village Soviet, the

bride's family and guests set out for the bridegroom's house, to which the couple would come from the Soviet. At the same time, the girls carried the bride's bedding over to the bridegroom's house. The bridegroom's parents "purchased" the dowry from the girls.

The young couple drove up to the house, and the bridegroom's parents met them at the gate in accordance with tradition. The bridegroom's mother poured grain over the pair, who tried to catch the kernels. "The number of kernels they catch is the number of children they will have," said the peasants. Women standing on the porch sang welcoming songs. The bride and bridegroom entered the house and sat down at the table, after which the guests were invited to take their places at the table. The wedding banquet began.

Everybody dances and sings at a wedding. The bride, the bridegroom, the matchmaker, and the guests are all tossed up into the air. This part of the ritual is filled with folk singing: The young couple and the guests all sing wedding songs.

Then the guests all left the bridegroom's house and went over to the bride's house, and in the evening everybody returned to the bridegroom's. As in the old days, the bed for the newlyweds was made up in the entry hall or the storage room.

The next day young women in masquerade came over from the bride's house to the bridegroom's. They danced and smashed pots and "searched for the young wife" or "heifer." Then the bride's parents arrived, and the matchmaker came with an omelet and a pie decorated with small coins. The omelet and the pie were placed on the table, and one of the guests grabbed the omelet and tried to run out into the street with it. The newlyweds are supposed to ransom it. In other variations, the bridegroom first sticks a fork into the omelet. The guests then place coins on the pie (this is called "silvering" the bride), and the bride takes this money for herself. Now it is also the custom to give the bride presents such as hosiery, perfume, cloth for a blouse, and dishes. In Bezhetsy District it is the custom to give joke-presents (rubber nipples, dolls, baby bathtubs, and the like) and to play a game called "mailman" in which the guests send the young couple comical messages of congratulation.

In some villages it is customary for the bride to give the bridegroom's family some gifts after the "silvering." She gives cloth for a dress to her mother-in-law, shirts to her father-in-law and the bridegroom, and towels to the other members of the family.

The guests tip the cook, who complains of fatigue and makes witty remarks in an effort to get larger tips.

Of the postwedding cycle, the custom of giving parties for the newlyweds has been preserved. The parties go on throughout the year, with all the relatives who attended the wedding giving them in turn. In some villages (Borovskoye, Sandovo District) they still follow the custom of ducking the young wife during the haymaking or at least splashing some water on her. This was thought to have magical power.

In all the districts we studied, the wedding ritual was basically the same, although nearly every village had variations of its own.

Old Bratsk

"The old city of Bratsk was built in 1631. Today it is covered by the man-made Bratsk Sea. There is a new Bratsk being built some twenty miles from the power station where there was nothing but taiga and wild animals before.

"For many people Bratsk is a preview of Siberia's future. What I noticed here is that Siberians in some ways resemble Texans, especially in their tendency to speak in superlatives. They like to say: '500 miles? That's nothing at all.' '100 rubles? That's not money.' 'A bottle of vodka? You don't call that a drink do you!'—all of which bears witness to their unharnessed pride in this gigantic area, which plays an ever more important role in the development of the country."

(Excerpts from *Soviet Life*, February, 1966)

New Bratsk

AN UNSENTIMENTAL VIEW

There are those who see the defense of the old peasant cultural life as a sentimental thing and counter it by emphasizing that what the village needs is an efficient modern agriculture. Here is an example of their thinking, from an article in the magazine Selskaya molodezh (Village Youth) *in February, 1969.*

Could it be that those who advocate restoring the old ways in rural life are right when they regret that the old songs are no longer sung and the round dances no longer danced in the villages, that the laments and rituals are being forgotten, and that the people are ceasing to be creators of beauty?

This kind of sentimental, romantic attitude toward our peasantry and its future has many attractions, especially for one who loves the land. The trouble is, however, that this attitude, for all its genuine love and respect for the peasantry, does not, for some reason, find a response in the hearts of those whom it concerns—the peasants.

You cannot get away from the fact that the spiritual, ethical, and everyday life of the old Russian village did not fall from the sky but was a consequence of the economics of peasant life, of the patriarchal noncommodity forms of agriculture. Even the aesthetics were determined by the peasant way of life, by the isolation and unchangeability of subsistence farming. It is no accident, for example, that up to the

Revolution the village of Kokshenga in Vologda Province was a veritable museum of folk art. Right up to the 1920's, Kokshenga, cut off from the world by forests and swamps and lacking means of communication, produced everything it needed with the exception of tea, vodka, and plowshares. That is the reason for the extraordinarily high level of its crafts—its woodcarvings, birchbark articles, printed textiles, embroidery—and the purity of its folk traditions and customs, which had been handed down from parents to children since Novgorod times. Yet a wedding held in Kokshenga last year in accordance with the old ritual that went back centuries— and Kokshenga is probably the only place in Vologda Province where such a wedding could have taken place—was in effect a theatrical production, with spectators, including writers and radio and newspaper reporters, coming from as far away as Vologda.

The disappearance of the old customs may be regrettable, but one cannot help seeing that it is the result of profound changes that have taken place in the psychology and character, and the entire way of life, of the peasantry—changes that have not been caused by anyone's subjective will but are due to real-life, objective causes.

Is this good or bad?

No one denies that the northern Russian countryside lived rather poorly in the postwar decades. But why? Was it because the village had departed from the patriarchal way of life, or was it because it had not arrived at what Lenin called industrial agriculture? What is the solution for the village today, to move backward or forward?

There is only one solution, and that is to organize a socialist industrial agriculture that is economically efficient.

A disapproving stare

PART SIX

Manners and Morals

Boys and girls in the Soviet Union have the same dating problems as elsewhere. But there are some ways in which these universal problems are faced a little differently because of the Russian experience. Many people in the outside world have an exaggerated notion of the "free love" aspect of the Russian Revolution. After a brief period in which all old traditions were questioned or overturned, the new regime asserted a puritanical attitude toward sexual morality and tried to strengthen family life in order to reduce juvenile delinquency and other consequences of broken homes. World War II also affected behavior patterns—it tragically unbalanced the number of males and females in the society and obliged many women to do men's work. Although this may have been a great gain for women's equality, it inevitably undermined the special treatment which—as can be seen from some of the following selections—women have ambivalent feelings about losing. Since the war, although abortions have been relatively easier than in many other countries, public discussion of sex and birth control has been quite inhibited. Young people are almost totally on their own in this sensitive area of life, and their behavior reflects this, ranging from ignorance and prudishness to an active sex life, with most girls still feeling constraints upon them. Unless they have wise parents with whom they can talk out their problems, the young have almost nowhere to turn to for guidance on this subject. There are no courses in the schools, virtually no books to consult, and only a few timid discussions in the press. This shying away from discussion is largely the feeling of a people still partly peasant in outlook that such things are best left to their natural development and that to talk about them publicly would create more problems than already exist. As Anton Makarenko, the famous teacher, once wrote, "No talks with children about the 'sex' problem can add anything to the knowledge that will come of itself in good time." Increasingly, this view has been challenged by people who feel that the absence of public discussion produces confusion and far too many casualties among the young, and these people are urging the inclusion of sex education in the school curriculum. The fact that sex is kept out of movies, television, and the press is one reason why the social life of young Russians is much slower to develop than it is here. Until well along in their teens, they go out and do things in groups rather than in couples—be it skating, going to a movie, or on an excursion into the countryside. Pairing off begins only in the last year or so of high school or after graduation. At that point, most youngsters suddenly find themselves out on their own, confronting the whole range of problems all at once and having to make their way to sexual maturity and marriage as best they can.

"LONG LIVE COURTEOUS MEN!"

How many hundreds of thousands of Russian girls must feel as this one does about the way boys treat them! But whereas most of them see no alternative and remain quiet, Alla had a brief glimpse of gallantry, and this stimulated her to express her feelings about upbringing in a letter to the magazine Yunost (Youth), *No. 4, 1968.*

Hello, there!

I'm not sorry that I went on the excursion. I have gotten more out of this week than out of ten years in school.

For the first time I felt like a member of the "weaker sex," and I enjoyed the feeling. I never imagined before how pleasant it is when somebody offers a hand to help you on or off the train, when he brings you a glass of water and helps you open the window (in trains they are very hard to open, you know). These are little things, but they are pleasant little things. I can't say that the boys in our class are terrible, but when I returned to it I was in a different world. I was no longer accustomed to the crush in the cafeteria, when the boys aggressively elbow their way in to grab a glass of tea. I was unaccustomed to not being greeted and to having a book snatched out of my hands.

Why didn't this behavior seem outrageous to me before?

In amazement, I shared my reaction with one of the girls in my class. She shrugged her shoulders and said with an ironic smile that this simply is the way people here are. But why? After all, the boys who went on the excursion with us are also from the schools of our city. In their schools, do they behave as our boys do? How unpleasant to think that once again I'll have to get used to the boys who don't let you pass and don't offer you a seat. And you know, it's the same in every grade, beginning with the first grade.

I have seen our boys act differently, but only with girls they like. They like one, and the others they push around and insult.

The most awful thing is that we've grown accustomed to all this. At seventeen, I already see the shortcomings of our upbringing.

There is something else I want to say. What do we know about classical music? Why do most of my classmates find it boring? Where is the ennobling influence of sports? Why do a lot of young people snicker when they see statues of nudes in the museums? Who is to blame for such attitudes? We should be breathing in culture like fresh air as early as kindergarten, and in school they should teach us not just physics and mathematics.

I am about to graduate from school, and only now have I learned that there are boys, younger and older, who will give up their seats to you in the bus and help you down from a high step.

Long live courteous men! I would like young men of my age to read this letter. They are pretty good kids—they'll understand what I mean.—Alla I., city of Khabarovsk.

THE COMPLICATED QUESTION

OF MODERN MANNERS

In 1967 the newspaper Komsomolskaya pravda (Young Communist League Truth) *held a discussion on the topic "What Are Contemporary Manners?" To judge by the published comments, the old view that it doesn't matter if a man has bad manners as long as he is good inside is no longer as widely held as in the early periods of Soviet Communism. Society in the cities has developed to the point where people are now concerned not only about the physical amenities of life but also about style, appearances, and behavior. Here are parts of the discussion, published on December 8, 15, and 29.*

Malakhovka, Moscow Province—I recently had occasion to take a night train. A girl was sitting diagonally across from me. She took a textbook out of a briefcase and began to read. I could not help admiring her. She had modesty, grace, and dignity.

Then a young man came into the coach. He was very nice-looking, too. He wore a stylish coat and was bareheaded. I watched to see where he would sit down. The boy inspected the coach with a quick, lively glance and, sure enough, sat down opposite the girl. I smiled to myself: Good for him, he saw beauty at once. Had I been younger, I would probably have done the same.

But what happened next? The young man plumped himself down on the seat, spread his legs apart and put one leg on the window ledge; he looked like someone sitting by a campfire. Then he yawned voluptuously, opening his mouth as wide as it would go. When he began to pick his teeth, then lifted his right leg even higher, I felt so uncomfortable that I got up and went into another coach.

I often wonder why, when noble and lofty deeds are by no means rare in our country, some of our young people have such—let's not mince words—barbaric manners?

Think about the young fellows who shuffle along the streets with their collars turned up and their caps stuck on the sides of their heads, chewing on cigarettes butts and spitting with relish. Think, girls, about how the boys you know call you "Ninka" and "Zinka" and "Lenka," how they hardly even look at you but just thrust out their hands when they ask you to dance, how they breathe right into your faces and their breath smells of vodka. Think, ladies, about how young men push you when you are in the street or on streetcars and laden with bundles. And they don't even bother to apologize.

But my main point is not these rather hackneyed illustrations. My main point goes much deeper. The lack of good manners among young people (and not only among the young!) and the inability to behave well in public actually discredit a person.

Someone may say: Don't you know that crude manners often conceal good hearts and, conversely, one can behave correctly yet be a bad person? Yes, I know this. Even more, I am sure that the majority of young people are better than would seem to be the case judging by their manners. Nevertheless, I'd like to reply to my opponents as follows.

We are about fifty years too late with the formula that "crude manners often conceal wonderful hearts." This is how the common people used to be depicted, with allowances for their ignorance and lack of education. Nowadays, to say condescendingly, "You know, he does have bad manners, but then he is so sincere, so direct, so aware" is to insult the young person in question.—V. Kvashnin, teacher.

Dnepropetrovsk—Hello, Komsomolka! I want to ask you a question that I often come up against and that bothers me.

The following incident recently took place after an amateur show at our plant's club. There were five of us, two boys and three girls. We went down to the cloakroom, and each of us put on his coat in the normal way, without pushing. Two elderly women were standing nearby and suddenly started scolding us: Why weren't we helping our "ladies"? We didn't argue with them. Not because we thought we were to blame, but because the exchange had greatly embarrassed "our ladies," and we did not want to cause them additional unpleasantness.

Why don't we help them into their coats? Is it so difficult for us? Don't we respect our girl friends? Nothing of the sort. It is precisely because we do respect them. The point is that life has changed, and so has the position of women in society. Women have become our equals in everything. So why must we bow and scrape unnecessarily as if in recognition that they are the "weak sex"?

Honestly, I myself have observed how such politeness can only insult and humiliate a woman. After all, she does the same work we do. Say she is a crane operator. Why should I treat her as if she were a china doll? I can show my respect for her better in some other way, in something genuine.

Yes, I'll give up my seat to an old woman or man because they really need it. But gallantry is personally repulsive to me. I am convinced that it can do nothing but insult any self-respecting woman. So tell me, am I wrong?—S. Merkulov.

Komsomolskaya pravda Editors' Note: Discussions of manners are as ancient as the world. But each new generation decides these questions for itself. As is evident from these two letters, the problem remains pertinent and disturbing. The people who wrote them are arguing with each other, though they have never seen each other and are not acquainted.

Let's think about this together: Do "chivalrous" manners conflict with genuine civic and spiritual qualities in young people? Is internal cultivation possible without external cultivation? Is gallantry obsolete?

Grozny—I do not understand S. Merkulov's hostility toward gallantry.

To spit at a fascist, to spit in the face of death—that is a just and correct way to manifest sincere, strong hatred and contempt for an enemy. But if a student at a higher school—but why a student?—sometimes even an older person—spits a cigarette butt onto the floor and carefully and precisely grinds it out with his fashionable shoe, that is indeed uncivilized, it shows a boorish attitude toward society.

However, there are reasons for reproaching girls too. I can understand that a woman who has lived through war or through great sorrow might smoke. But it is most unpleasant to see a very young girl take a cigarette after a glass of wine (or even vodka!) and inhale arrogantly, like a man. For her, smoking is not yet a need but merely an affectation that spoils her.

Some girls, especially in the big cities, have recently begun to affect a deliberate rudeness and abruptness. Girls, for all your equality with us men, stay feminine, gentle, and weak (in the best, Marxist sense of this concept), stay beautiful not only internally but also in your manners. Do not delude yourselves and us.

I am for politeness, for gallantry.—V. Kurgansky, graduate student.

First of all, in discussing the culture of behavior it is utterly absurd to use such a concept as the equality of men and women. The error in S. Merkulov's "Amazon" theory is that in recognizing woman's right to wear overalls, he refuses her the right to elementary human consideration. So I disagree absolutely with S. Merkulov's utterly strange opinion.—V. Malukhin, student at Moscow State University.

Rovno—In carrying "What Are Contemporary Manners?" the newspaper has raised a truly urgent problem. It is, I think, troubling all members of the younger generation. Discussions of rules of conduct have often appeared in newspapers, but they have been extremely superficial, in my opinion, on the principle: "Say this, say that, and then forget it." And afterward some elderly person asks: "Where do young people get their bad manners?" In such cases I feel like asking in sorrow: Where are they to get better manners?

There are no special magazines or literature on this important subject. Nor can one always depend on the knowledge of one's elders. It is fine if parents possess natural tact and pass it on to their children. But this does not happen in all families. Of course, elementary rules of behavior are ingrained, so to speak, in every person, but this is far from enough. Few young people know how to carry on a conversation, how to set a table, how to introduce acquaintances (if there are more than two or three), how to entertain them. For some reason only the *Magazine of Fashions* has devoted adequate space to the problem of manners, but it has a very limited circulation and cannot always be obtained.

Last year I visited Czechoslovakia, and I must say much more attention is paid there to these problems. In many cities I saw posters announcing that dance schools were admitting pupils, and in Prague a School of Good Taste had been opened. Experienced teachers and specialists in good manners give instruction in such subjects as physical education (posture, the aesthetics of movement); aesthetic education (principles of aesthetics, acquaintance with the culture of modern man's environment); taste in everyday matters and the ability to dress well; lessons in good manners, makeup, and hygiene.

The question of modern manners is very complicated and cannot be settled in a few newspaper articles. Why not deal with it seriously and on a countryside scale? Why not start a magazine called *Good Manners* (for example), that is, a sort of Soviet school of good taste? If this matter is not tackled in earnest we shall have plenty of time to marvel at people who still have extremely primitive ideas about the decorum of social intercourse.—Zh. Petrenko.

Moscow—You're quite right, esteemed Comrade Merkulov, times have changed, and equality has become a great blessing for Soviet women. It's too bad, however, that many of our men interpret this too freely. Equality, as they see it, means a woman makes breakfast in the morning, takes the children to the nursery, and then runs off to work. In the evening everything is done in reverse order: the nursery, the kitchen stove, the laundry.

I'm not advocating putting man at the washtub, or handing him a mop. But how often, in this daily kitchen whirlpool, a woman misses the male gallantry and even simple tenderness that could give her fresh strength and banish her weariness.

I'm not a classic example of the "weak sex," the "china doll." I used to go in for sports, running twenty to thirty kilometers daily in training with the fellows, and I was none the worse for it. Still, it was pleasant when one of them casually took my skis and carried them to the bus stop. No matter how strong and equal a woman might be, she always likes to lean on a reliable arm. This feeling must have been given to us by nature.

That is why I shall never disdain a gallantly proffered coat in a cloakroom, or a helping hand as I get off a bus. As for flowers? In your eyes, Comrade Merkulov, are they an insult to us, too? But I'd like to see the woman who doesn't like this prerogative of the "weak sex"!—N. Taprova, landscaping engineer.

Brovary—I'm eighteen years old. I was born in a remarkably beautiful area, the Transcarpathians.

I am interested in radio and movie equipment, cybernetics, photography, literature, and foreign languages and am attracted to people with inquiring minds.

From the Transcarpathians I went to Kiev and later to Brovary, where I live now. I got acquainted with a girl, wanted to be friends with her, share my thoughts with her, and read poetry to her, but I soon noticed that she was not interested.

In talking to the fellows who live at the dormitory with me, I learned that they had had the same experience. I'm coming increasingly to the conclusion that many girls just want an easy, carefree life, they are out to get married as soon as they can for the sake of their own comfort. I've seen some of the fellows bring girls to their quarters and drink vodka with them.

What's surprising is that the girls hear coarse words and cursing, but they are not in the least indignant; they're resigned to it. And the fellows think that that's as it should be. This is why their courtesy and chivalrous attitudes toward women are vanishing. The girls are to blame for all this. My friends and I have reached this conclusion. Could I be wrong? —Yu. Monyak.

FIFTEEN BOYS

Bella Akhmadulina, an outstanding woman poet, wrote this about 1959, when she was twenty-two years old. It appeared in English in The New Russian Poets, 1953 to 1966, *edited and translated by George Reavey.*

Fifteen boys and, maybe, more,
or fewer than fifteen, maybe,
said to me
in frightened voices:
"Let's go to a movie or the Museum of Fine Arts."
I answered them more or less like this:
"I haven't time."
Fifteen boys presented me with snowdrops.
Fifteen boys in broken voices
said to me:
"I'll never stop loving you."
I answered them more or less like this:
"We'll see."

Fifteen boys are now living a quiet life.
They have done their heavy chores
of snowdrops, despair and writing letters.
Girls love them—
some more beautiful than me,
others less beautiful.

Fifteen boys with a show of freedom, and at times spite,
salute me when we meet,
salute in me when we meet,
their liberation, normal sleep and regular meals.

In vain you come to me, last boy.
I shall place your snowdrops in a glass of water,
and silver bubbles will cover
their stocky stems . . .
But, you see, you too will cease to love me,
and, mastering yourself, you'll talk in a superior way,
as though you'd mastered me,
and I'll walk off down the street, down the street . . .

(Translated by George Reavey)

HOW FAR

SHOULD A GIRL GO?

In 1968, after running an article on love and sex, Komsomolskaya pravda (Young Communist League Truth) received a flood of letters from readers. The editors sent a batch over to Lev Kassil, who writes for and about young people, and asked him to come up with some wise counsel. It was no easy task, even for such an adroit writer. Here is part of one of the letters, followed by excerpts from Kassil's reply, which appeared in the newspaper on January 10, 1969.

Perhaps it is absurd to write about such things in the newspaper, but I beg of you, I very much beg you to answer me. I know a girl who once said, "I really envy girls who have experienced everything (who have gone through fire and water). I too would very much like to do this, but I don't have enough courage."

At the time I was dumbfounded by this. You really need courage to have experienced everything by the age of eighteen or twenty.

They say we ourselves are to blame, that we have been too easy with the boys and have spoiled them. Is this true?

I don't want to be touched by the hands of somebody who has not yet become dear to me—I don't want to belong to somebody just casually. How many times boys have dropped me only because I was an "untouchable." Just now I broke up with someone very dear to me who is far from being a boy and who wanted too much from me.

All this is painful, very painful. Sometimes you even think, well, am I perhaps really a fool? But if you stumble once, then it will be so easy to slide down. And I really want to believe that I will find a man who will love me with his heart and will understand me.

Tell me, what should I do? I am desperate. I can't consult with Mama because, on the whole, she is a stranger to me. Excuse me, I understand that there are more important matters, but please answer me.

From Lev Kassil's answer:

I must confess that it was very hard for me to write about all this. There are things that are more easily said face to face. But how can I talk in private with each one of those who sent letters (and there were hundreds of them) on a subject that for some reason our press is not much in the habit of mentioning. It is not every mother who can bring herself to talk frankly about this subject even with her own daughter. And still less do you hear such a conversation in the high school classroom or the university lecture hall.

And the matter troubles everyone, especially, of course, the young. It is not for nothing that the "conversation about a girl's honor" on the pages of *Komsomolskaya pravda* brought forth such a voluminous outpouring of agitated readers' letters. The responses were various. Both girls and boys wrote. They wrote with emotion, at times polemically, but almost always sincerely, openly, and demanding a reply. I read with interest dozens of these letters that were made available to me by the editors of the newspaper.

> *Kassil's article offered generalities on the safe side, advising the young not to be in any hurry to*

start sexual relations until they felt real and last-
ing love for each other. He came down hard on
Soviet men who still hold the "double-standard"
view that they can do as they please with women,
and equally hard on modern Western ideas about
sex.

No, the girl who wrote the letter should not reproach
herself as if she had acted stupidly. She is young, only nineteen, and of course she is still going to meet a man who will
be more solicitous and kind to her. She has only to know
how to wait while holding to high standards. And of course
the girl is right to repel the shameless boys who badger her,
to oblige them to hold their tongues and keep their hands to
themselves. When they have gotten what they deserve, let
them go on and wax eloquent about the idea that maidenly
honor became outmoded a long time ago and about how it
is now "unfashionable to be a virgin." Fashions have a short
life, whereas real love is for a long time!

I have here some more letters from other cities and villages,
and in them I also read, "He said it's no longer fashionable
to be a virgin."

Crudeness and caddishness, displaying impudent force
against a woman, showing brazen scorn for the feeling of
womanly modesty, insulting a girl's and a woman's honor—
these are loathsome in the extreme, and there can be no ex-
cusing such things in our society. Some boys have a filthy and
disgusting attitude toward girls—these vulgar young feather-
brains regard them as just an object for diversion. . . .

Do they really know what the great sacred happiness of
love is—those who lustfully and hurriedly grab the small joys
in flight. This goes by a completely different name. Let all
those foreign "hippies" who hang gaudy, jingling necklaces
on themselves and don wilted garlands and brightly colored
rags—let them make themselves out to be people who have
returned to a primitive freedom of love. Having seen them

more than once on the streets of Western Europe and America, we have noticed what sad confusion and cold emptiness are concealed in their deliberately wild appearances and reckless ways. Raving as if possessed, they howl about free love, but in reality they are condemning lofty human feelings to servitude for the pleasure of public fashion. Genuine freedom should not be confused with tarnished license. What does this have to do with fashion, anyway? You may wear miniskirts, yet need not doom yourself to shamefully shortened mini-feelings that expose primitive needs.

> *Kassil's article brought another wave of some 1,500 letters, which became the basis of still another discussion in* Komsomolskaya pravda *on February 23, 1969. This girl's letter, the newspaper said, was "rather typical of the reactions."*

Hello, People!

I don't agree with Lev Kassil. In my opinion, if you have come to love someone (not "fallen in love," God help us, it's a despicable term!)—then go ahead and love! Lose your head. Lose a great deal irretrievably, a very great deal. Be happy. But afterward, don't cry, don't whimper. Be true to your love. Don't squander it!!!

I was once happy. And even though I'm alone now, I don't want any other kind of happiness in exchange. It may have been bitter and fleeting and obtained at a high price, but it was happiness! And neither being admitted to Moscow University nor having an interesting job can compare with such happiness. It was three years ago, but it seems like today. —Tatyana

> *Tatyana's letter was perhaps the most definite statement about sex in a discussion that roamed unsystematically and vaguely over the field, never really coming to grips with the subject. The one point on which many people seem to agree and*

176 §   MANNERS AND MORALS

> *express themselves unequivocally, both in this dis-*
> *cussion and elsewhere in the Soviet press, is that*
> *the continuing public reluctance to talk about sex*
> *openly and intelligently is a disservice to the*
> *young people.*

Both in school and at home, we really are brought up in absolute ignorance. I, for example, can't remember a single instance in my childhood or as a teenager when an adult talked to me about this subject.

Yes, unpardonably little, intolerably superficially, do we talk about such subjects with our young people!

How can such ignorance be combated if the teacher, the parent, and even the young married couple themselves cannot find a single bookstore with a brochure that explains these questions in an elementary form?

Why do they keep silent about this? Why wait until somebody makes a mistake, after which you can shrug your shoulders and say, "Well, people learn from mistakes."

MARINA GETS A LECTURE

*In September, 1969, Yunost (Youth) carried an
anguished cry for help from a girl named Marina.
The response by a woman journalist is interesting for what it reveals of popular attitudes. During and after the war, when men were in short
supply, many women had no alternative but to
go ahead and have a child out of wedlock, and
both public opinion and the leadership accepted
this as the reality of the time. Now that the
ratio of young men to young women has returned to normal, the society once again frowns
on unwed motherhood. Abortions are legal and
cheap, and many women resort to them, for the
contraceptives on sale up until now have been
of unreliable quality. The "pill" has not been
available to the public; Soviet doctors say they
are concerned about its possible dangerous effects
on the body and that instead they will rely on
nonchemical means of contraception. You will
notice that the response to Marina doesn't even
mention contraceptives as a way of avoiding her
predicament—reflecting an uneasiness about this
whole subject and perhaps even a fear that, if
contraceptives become reliable and widely used,
they may lead to much greater sexual freedom
for the young, similar to what has come about
in the West.*

Dear *Yunost!*

I have never written any letters to the editor, but I can no longer bear it. I have to tell someone about my grief.

You probably receive other letters like this, and you won't care about me. Still, I will try to explain what happened.

I had a boyfriend. Everything was fine with us for some time. And then. I don't even know how to write about this. He stopped coming to see me. It's hard for me to tell you what I suffered—I felt it wasn't worth living any longer.

After a while I began a life of constantly going out with various boys. To be frank with you, it makes no difference to me who they are, whether they are good or bad. I have gotten so accustomed to all this that I don't know what will become of me. I tried to talk with my friends about it, but they all laugh at me. They say that the same thing has happened to them too. And that there is nothing terrible about it, because it's the kind of time we live in and everybody is that way.

Now I am going to have a baby. I haven't told anybody yet. And I'm not even seventeen.

Is it really true that all girls are this way?

If possible, please print my letter. At least somebody reply to me. Young people too. I'm ashamed to write my last name and address. I beg for your help.—Marina

The main question, which Marina did not ask, is this: Why is it bad to "go out with," as she calls it, to have intimate relations with many different men? Let us try to reason practically, on a level that seems contemporary to Marina and her friends. The most practical answer to the question is that from intimacy with a man, a woman can have a child.

Let us put aside moral concepts for the moment. You can go around turning up your nose and spitting at public opinion and can consider yourself a very modern girl, until such time as your relations with "various boys" lead to their natural outcome, until, as they expressed it in the old days, you are carrying a baby under your heart.

Just being pregnant for nine months without a husband is difficult. A woman in this condition needs male support in the most direct sense: Someone has to do for her the physical work that previously she easily managed by herself. Moreover, the same moral concepts that it was so pleasant to scorn now turn against you. You suffer—you cannot but suffer—from the condemning glances of your neighbors, from the reproaches and tears of your mother. In the maternity home, you are tormented by the letters and flowers that have been sent to the other women by their husbands.

I know some women who have endured all this with dignity; I respect those women and even admire them: In order to have the very great joy of motherhood, they have gathered all their courage. Life, with all its complexities, does not bestow on everyone easy and harmonious happiness —it may happen that a woman loves a married man who cannot leave his family; it may happen that she loves a man who is unworthy; it also may happen that a woman decides to have a child by a man she doesn't love, because she dreams of having a child, the years are going by, and there is no one she loves.

But what has Marina got to do with any of these situations? Did she really want a child? Or is she prepared to bring it up? What can she teach the child, for what sort of life can she prepare it—for one such as she herself led? So that by the age of seventeen, her child is "ashamed to give its last name"?

However, Marina's friends, who think "all girls are that way," are very well acquainted with another way out: To get pregnant is no misfortune—you can have an abortion in any hospital. "Of course," they say, "it's unpleasant. People find out about it and there are rumors. But still, it's better than having the child."

It may be that the whole matter is effectively settled and that in a few years this ultra-modern girl finds herself a husband and happily has a baby. But it can turn out other-wise—even though not always. When she becomes mature and feels an irresistible craving for motherhood, a woman may pay the most terrible price for not having wanted to give birth in her first pregnancy: She is not able to have any more children. Such is the price of irresponsibility.

Try and tell me that at sixteen you don't know this. That you don't know where babies come from and you don't know that to destroy your first baby is dangerous. You know all these things, and you don't give any thought to them.

PREPARATION FOR THE

KINGDOM OF LOVE

Those who favor sex education for the young support their argument with statistics from the divorce courts and studies that have recently been made of marital problems. E. Kostyashkin, of the Academy of Pedagogical Sciences, has written often on the subject, and here are some of his remarks from Pravda *on November 18, 1968.*

The unhappy marriages of those who graduated from school in the early postwar years seemed explainable to some extent. Some young men and women failed the "endurance test" in complex situations that involved the difficulties of living with parents or in dormitories and of placing children in nurseries and kindergartens.

But how is one to explain the fact that, although the material position and well-being of families substantially improved, the parents' cultural level rose, and their needs for preschool institutions were essentially met, many of my former pupils have not found happiness in marriage?

The more family and marriage problems I see among my pupils, the more sharply I feel guilty toward them. We pedagogues instilled in them a love of labor, books, and civic work, but we did not teach them how to behave in everyday life, in their marriages, and with their children.

We failed to teach Andrei how to understand people, and he was conquered by the very first flutters of some good-for-nothing woman's false eyelashes; Nina was not taught how to balance a budget; Natasha wasn't told how to bring up children.

According to data from a sample study, the majority of young parents complain that the child appeared "a little too soon."

"Seryozha prevented me from finishing the institute."

"Yes, we weren't really in a hurry. After all, we are both studying, and we still don't have a room."

This is the most "classic" revelation: "We didn't want the child, but he was born anyway." In a general sense, the appearance of an heir has given joy to young parents—but only until the first nocturnal howl. What is this, a lack of understanding of what marital relations can lead to? Or complete ignorance of physiological matters? Most likely, both.

In our opinion, it would be worth while for pedagogues, together with medical men, to develop, finally, a course in sex education for secondary school. Discussions of this problem have had a peculiar vogue in the press. But for the time being everything remains unchanged.

The concentration of the teachers' attention on academic problems in the senior classes is completely understandable. But it is inadmissible to overlook young people's personal lives because of that. After all, not a single one of our charges will escape the magical kingdom of love. And they should enter that kingdom well prepared.

UNINFORMED OPINIONS

Here are two glimpses of popular attitudes that may help readers to understand why the advocates of sex education in the schools have made so little headway up until now in getting their proposals accepted. The first is from a letter in Komsomolskaya pravda *(Young Communist League Truth) on February 23, 1969, by a Hungarian boy studying at Leningrad University who was astounded by what one of his Russian friends said. The second, in* Yunost *(Youth), No. 3, 1968, presents the views of some readers about art reproductions of nudes.*

I was astonished when a girl told me about an "awful incident": A boy kissed her! She nearly fainted, quite literally. She got terribly frightened because she thought she would have a baby! (From a kiss.)

Then I asked her, "Didn't you study biology in school?" Answer: "When we got to that part of the course, I preferred to play sick and not go to class rather than listen to and talk about such vulgar things . . ."

Of course, this attitude grows out of an incorrect upbringing.

"What conclusion will our young people draw when they look at this picture?" three readers from Moldavia ask in a letter to *Yunost.* "Couldn't you think of anything more interesting to print?" is the ironic inquiry of a reader who wishes to remain anonymous. A woman reader in Murmansk formulated her question to the magazine as follows: "Should pupils look at such a picture, and what ideas would it leave in their minds?"

What did the magazine do, what mistake did it perpetrate?

We rummaged through last year's file and found the May issue. It contained several reproductions of paintings that had been hung at exhibitions of Moscow and Russian Federation artists. It was the readers' opinion that one of these paintings, *Sun, Air, and Water,* by the artist A. April, should not have been carried in *Yunost.*

Three nude girls are shown on the bank of a river. It is a lonely spot, and the girls felt they could bathe nude. In our

The offending painting, entitled *Sun, Air, and Water*

(*Yunost,*
May, 1967)

view, the artistic treatment of the subject is irreproachable: Everything is very charming, pure, modest. But readers are angry. What is the matter?

Here is another letter, written by reader M. at the request

of a group of patients in a hospital in Ust-Donetsk Settlement, Rostov Province. They too are displeased with *Yunost* for carrying the reproduction of April's painting, and are also displeased with the magazine *Ogonyok*. What has *Ogonyok* done? Let these readers speak for themselves, in their own style: "It shows a full-length front view of the sculpture *The Dancer*. Like me, many of the patients are surprised and dismayed by such works of realism: After all, our children too look at illustrated magazines." These readers go on to report that in the West there are "clubs for the dissipated and the idle" where guests are served by waitresses who are stark naked and where nude paintings or sculpture would be quite appropriate. "But in our country we have no such clubs, and we consider the depiction of naked women unwarranted."

For example, take the reader N.: Her fourth question shows unconcealed wrath: "What were you printing in your magazine, anyway?" And the fifth falls like a whiplash: "A page of lewdness, depravity and swinishness?" N. knows exactly where such pages lead: "This is where young people get their willfulness, licentiousness, and obscenity!"

She informs us that "my generation was raised without displays of such paintings and drawings."

TWO YOUNG MARRIAGES

Here are portraits of two young marriages—the problems that developed in them and the results that ensued. The first is a student couple, and the article alternates reports on them with some general observations about student marriages. In the second piece, the author has his eye on the generational differences, especially between the women of the family. As you will see, the differences are striking, and the young Soviet wife emerges as quite a modern woman.

The wedding took place in the dormitory in a small room temporarily loaned to the newlyweds by its two student occupants. There were straw-covered bottles of Gamza [Bulgarian red wine] on the table, and apples and potato salad —nothing fancy of course, but we felt good.

Liuba and I looked at the bride with a complex feeling of joy and sadness and a touch of pity, and I kept recalling a verse that is beloved for its faint note of just such despairing, plaintive poetry—the poetry of someone else's wedding.

"I want to be a bride, beautiful and with curled hair, beneath a modest white veil."

"Well now," I said, when it was my turn to propose a toast, "let's drink to our hope that the bride will always be as gay and pretty and slender as she is now."

"Tell her how you managed to do it," somebody said to me, and everyone roared with laughter.

The bride began to imagine out loud what her life would

be like. "I don't see how I could ever quarrel with him," said Tanka.

We did not say anything, but somehow we all believed that for these two young people, life would indeed be good.

At ten thirty in the evening, the dorm superviser intruded into our midst. She was a polite but inflexible woman. At first we did not understand why she had come, and then it became clear: the local authorities were throwing us out "under the regulations for the use of the dormitory."

We went out into the lighted night-time street, leaving Tanya and Volodya in the room that did not belong to them. We knew that they had ten kopeks between the two of them to get to their classes tomorrow—hers at one end of Moscow and his at the other. You see, we too were students at that time.

Student weddings, after all, are something special. Students are not fond of official festivity. They prefer to register their marriage in an ordinary ZAGS [government registry] office instead of in a wedding palace.

But people interfere with the celebration of weddings; they say, go to a restaurant and do it there. Well what if a student feels like celebrating his marriage in his dormitory room or in the cafeteria of his institute. In the Moscow Institute of Fine Chemical Technology there is a regulation forbidding the celebration of marriages, anniversaries, and birthdays in the dormitory. A fourth-year student, K., decided to risk it and had her wedding party in her own room. The result was that she got a written reprimand signed by the head of the institute. In student life there are many such "documents" of instructions, and other severities of all kinds.

During the last three years I have seen Tanya and Volodya often. I will select a few instances from our encounters.

Somehow I heard that they had had a baby.

I used to see Tanya by accident at the bus stop or in the subway. In my clever, beautiful Tanya's hand there was always a bedraggled yellow string bag. She had changed a great deal; she looked as if she had not had enough sleep for a long time.

"You know," she said at one of our meetings, "I'm tired of living on a student allowance. I don't think Volodya understands that, after all, he has to support his family. Maybe I'm wrong—of course he has to finish the institute, but then so do I. For some reason we have begun to quarrel."

One could already sense in her the emotional confusion that comes to very young people when everything in their lives, which they have beautifully arranged and planned for years ahead, suddenly tumbles down with a flick of the fingernail, like a house of cards.

They say the student family is ephemeral: it lives on goodness knows what and makes ends meet with incidental earnings (the student allowance is not enough). After all, it's youth and love we're talking about here, and for them all disorders are especially painful.

As soon as Tanya failed her first exam, they cut off her allowance. I think married students who have a child should receive an allowance no matter what happens. If young parents don't cope with their studies, then dismiss them from the institute or give them leave for a while, but if they are studying, they have to have something to live on (you know, it's harder for them than for the others).

There is another complication. Our young men have not been taught to understand that they must support their families. Especially the students. A worker has a better understanding of the few very simple fundamentals of life. The students have absorbed very well that we have equality, that everything is on equal grounds—the student wife does not disdain to scrub floors for money, but her husband does not always realize that he should take responsibility for a large part of the everyday difficulties. Here is a paradox: The head of the family doesn't understand that he must feed his family.

It seems as though you can learn to understand these things only by personal experience. Perhaps not only personal experience? Perhaps. But they give the student nothing but "popular-science" lectures on love and marriage, and they try in vain to get him to attend a discussion on the rather strange topic of "a girl's pride and a man's dignity."

I was once in their home; they had a rented room in someone's apartment. I came to Tanya in the evening and the two of us sat there until late at night. There were diapers hanging all over the room: the landlady did not let her hang them either in the bathroom or in the kitchen.

We talked about the institute. The whole room—the table, the window sill, the chairs—was covered with open books, but you could feel that Tanya was not touching them. She tried to study in the evening when the baby slept, yet she didn't make any progress and the year was wasted. Tanya was alone for days at a time. Volodya had some kind of important community work, and at night he had to earn money, so he came home very late—sleepy, tired, and irritable.

And I heard the words that have been heard a hundred times from others. "Listen, why does he think I always have to be the one to get up when the baby cries at night?"

Volodya came home after eleven. He wanted to sit and talk with us, but he had an exam in the morning and had to study. He spread out his books, and Tanya and I went into the kitchen. Ten minutes later, Tanya glanced into the room and beckoned to me with her finger: Volodya's head lay on his books and he was sleeping.

She wakened him and said, "Tomorrow, you stay with the baby. I have to study for my English exam."

"No," he replied, "I've already missed so many classes. How come you don't understand that my plans to get into graduate school are melting away."

"And how is it you don't understand that for me everything is melting away!"

They suddenly remembered that they were not alone.

"Who if not we ourselves turn our loved ones into such people, whom we no longer have the strength to love?" (That is not Shakespeare, but Yevtushenko.)

In Volodya's institute there were no children's nurseries at all, and in Tanya's there was a long waiting list. Some misunderstanding existed between them and their parents, so it was not possible to leave the child with the grandparents, as many of Tanya's friends did.

Yes, the children of students are an eternal problem.

For example, in the First Moscow Medical Institute there was a whole group of students who took turns looking after a baby until he became a little bigger, and each student worked to make up the lost time. This is wonderful of course, but you don't envy the child who each day was left with someone he didn't know, a new and inexperienced person. The institute has no nursery, only a kindergarten where they take children at the age of three. Don't you think this is precisely the reason why students so often have to place their babies in a home for infants. For whom is the kindergarten intended, if it accepts children only at the age of three? For the children of teachers and, at best, graduate students. While undergraduates manage to finish their studies with a child on their hands before it reaches the age of three.

In Moscow's Lenin Pedagogical Institute, there are neither nurseries nor kindergartens (and 87 per cent of the students are women).

Nurseries in the universities and institutes—that is one of the most important problems of the student family.

For the time being, while the students themselves have to sit with their children, young mothers should be allowed to have an individually worked out schedule of classes and examinations. Even this doesn't exist.

One day, having left her son with a friend, Tanya ran to the Komsomol committee to see if it would give her child a place in the nursery. One of the committee members received her in his office. He had the look of a person who understood everything, who even knew it all ahead of time and saw in her fate a "general institute" problem toward which he had a very complex attitude. He appeared to be an intelligent man and aroused confidence. Having heard Tanya out, he said, "You see, I think students in the first years of the university and institute should not get married. Maybe this sounds crude, but it really gets in the way of studying. And our task, after all, is to train specialists. Married students make bad specialists: when a student has to work as a night watchman and tend the baby and think all the time about money, he can't do a good job studying. In general, I think one should get married while still in university—there is more choice there—but not before the fourth year. The end is in sight, and even if you have a baby in your last year, it isn't terrible then. But whenever I hear about some first-year students getting married, frankly speaking, I feel sad."

"Excuse me," said Tanya, "I'm sorry that the echoes of life have touched your refined ears."

The last time we went to visit Tanya and Volodya was when everything had already settled down and stabilized. Volodya had graduated from the institute and was about to leave for his assigned job.

Tanya still had a year of study. Things were calm in their home and so were they. Tanya talked about her thesis and her research (she had just returned from a field trip, gathering folklore in Stavropol Territory), and we could feel that she was not upset either by the fact that Volodya hadn't received a very good job or by the fact that she would remain there alone. And from the way Tanya addressed herself to us and not to her husband, you could tell that by now it was easier for them to talk about anything at all with other people than it was to talk with each other.

For half a day I tried to track down by telephone the people who look after the problems of the student family. I became convinced that there is no one who looks after them. Studies, science, extracurricular activities, even art, even sport, even the KVN [quiz teams that compete among themselves]—everywhere people were able to give me exhaustive information about these things. But the family? "No, we can't do everything, after all."

In most of our universities and institutes, the Komsomol and other community organizations and the rectors think that there are community matters (again, studies and sports) and then there are personal matters (families, for example).

From one Komsomol leader I heard the following: "All the problems of the student family turn upon the problem of housing. This problem is so far insoluble, so there is nothing to write about." That is a typical prejudice. Why does it depend only on housing? I won't repeat what I've already said, but there is a lot that can be done.

Then they got a divorce. The official procedures took a long time: In the courtroom they were surprised that Tanya and Volodya had had no brawls and didn't abuse each other, and for that reason everyone considered it a sacred duty to try and reconcile them. Finally the documents had all been officially stamped. They went out into the street (it was late autumn and snowing) and walked down the long river bank where it was growing dark—not arm in arm, but side by side, and silent. Strangely enough, they had invited friends to their divorce.

The empty Poplavok [a floating restaurant] was rocking on the black water. We went in and sat down by the window at a long table meant for a large party of people. Tanya and Volodya didn't sit side by side as they usually did, but on opposite sides.

There was a clinking of glasses, and Tanya said, "Remember? In Pushkinsky."

I don't know what he was supposed to remember, but it was clear that, as always, he understood right away what she meant. And it seemed to me that none of this had happened yet, that it was all still in the future.

We sat there a long time—we had nowhere to hurry to—and those words kept coming back to me, "I want to be a bride, beautiful and with curls."

Komsomolskaya pravda (*Young Communist League Truth*), January 13, 1968

We are eternally in debt to our mothers, but the world is organized in such a way that what we owe our parents we give to our own children when we become parents.

Of course our sacrifice is already of a different order, more rational and moderate—I won't try to explain why. At any rate, in all her forty-nine years Maria Osipovna did not once go to a vacation resort and had never been outside her native region—she never even had the desire to. Slava and Irina, on the other hand, went to Moscow twice in one year. When I asked Irina if she wanted a second child, her answer was affirmative: Yes, she did, but only in five years' time. Why five years? Well, because she and Slava still had to finish their studies and have themselves a good time. That is how she put it: "to have a good time. There'll still be plenty of time left for looking after children."

Of course you would not hear such an answer from Maria Osipovna, but then her heart is put together according to an old recipe.

Once upon a time, getting married meant for a woman a complete ban on so-called "personal life." It meant you had to sit at home, no dances for you, no having a good time. It was altogether different for the husband, who, as it were, placed on his wife the chains that were lifted from himself. To the husband everything was permitted. But recently, Irina deposited her two-year-old daughter in a nursery, left her dear husband Slava, and calmly went off on a tourist trip to Poland. Maria Osipovna didn't say a word to her daughter-in-law, neither before she left nor after her return, but the atmosphere in the family was strained. "In our time," the mother reflected about herself, "we didn't dump our children in nurseries." "In your time," Irina reflected, "there were no nurseries."

Fortunately, on the most important questions, the elder Polyanovs display a touching unity; even if they quarrel, they do it in such a way that the children will not hear them and will continue to have the same regard for them.

Relations within the young mariages are taking shape differently, especially with Irina and Slava. They are also parents, although recent ones, and their basic conflicts are "formative" ones that stem mainly from Irina's desire to assert herself in the family.

When he got his pay, Slava often went out drinking with his friends, not because he enjoyed drinking but because he could not say no. Irina, of course, objected, and it wasn't at all for the sake of saving money—the reader will soon understand this. At first, she went to the factory entrance, where many of the women gathered, and accompanied her husband home. Their friends laughed, as one might expect, and Irina wept and started noisy quarrels in front of everyone, on the staircase, yelling at the top of her voice. She was, as Maria Osipovna put it, "a decent girl, but bold." And the neighbors, as everyone knows, are capable of adding ten words of their own to every word they hear. The whole family really felt for Slava and his shaky honor. He calmed his wife down as best he could and said to her, "Don't scream, people are listening," but it made no difference—she was a real "Italian" type. "To hell with them," she would scream. "You are the one I care about."

However long or short a time this went on, by the time

I got to know the Polyanovs, a "new life" had already triumphed in their family. On the day he got his pay, Slava put on a white shirt and a bright tie, well pressed (by him, I note in parentheses), gray trousers, a brown jacket with a beige handkerchief jutting out of the pocket, black loafers whose heels he had had cut into a conical shape—at Irina's insistence—and, together with his wife, who put on a little lipstick, went off to a restaurant.

Boris Yefimovich [Slava's father] contemptuously called the restaurant a "'restoratsia' where gilded ladies walk around practically naked." He just couldn't understand that a restaurant is not necessarily a place to get drunk in, that it can be a place where you listen to music, dance, look at people, and are seen by them. Watching his son leave, he peered at him over the top of his glasses as if to say that his son had fallen so low he had hit rock bottom.

Today in Slava's family there is "no division between man and woman," as Irina put it. It was hard to achieve that; it meant breaking with character and tradition, yet Irina achieved it, and now she and her husband do everything together—they go out on the town together, and keep house and look after their daughter together. While Slava did the marketing, Irina hammered a metal cornice into the wall. She did it badly, of course, but even here they were equal, since the dinners that Slava prepared were sometimes oversalted. Never mind, they ate them and laughed. It is interesting that Slava did not conceal his kitchen concerns from his neighbors. He walked proudly and did not attempt to hide the string bag he carried out of the Deluxe, as the nearest store was called. He considered equality to be fair and just, because he had learned a simple truth: If you do good to your wife, life will be better for you.

Do you hear this, men?

Komsomolskaya pravda,
May 15, 16, 17, 1969

PART SEVEN

Pacifism, Patriotism, and War

There is nothing that Russians feel more passionate about than the subject of war and peace. World War II is still a living memory for them, in part because so many families have gaps left by those who died and in part because the memory is kept alive by a flood of novels, stories, plays, movies, personal memoirs, and historical documents on the war that has been running high ever since the late 1950's. The young people have by now heard so much about the war that they must at times have the sensation of having lived through it themselves.

For all this, it is striking that the kind of anti-war sentiment that one sees among the young in other countries is not manifest in Soviet youth in the same way. To some extent, this is because the Soviet military men have been concerned that the expression of pacifism might weaken youth's patriotism and obedience, and they have taken steps to control it. Another reason is that Soviet youth—and the Soviet people as a whole—are less well informed about the nature of the contemporary arms race. There are no public discussions over there comparable to our debates on the ABM and MIRV. The Soviet press does not discuss Russia's very latest weapons—not even *the country's leading scientists know much about them, unless they work for the military, and there is not the same rotation in and out of high government posts that has helped to create in the United States a sizable group of people outside the military who are knowledgeable about weapons and are trying to educate the public about them. Russians often learn more about their country's military development by reading the Western press—those few who have access to it—than they do from Soviet sources.*

What the controlled Soviet press reflects are two sets of feelings within the country: the abhorrence of war (which is as strong in the Soviet people as in any people on earth) and, cutting across this, the efforts of those in authority who feel the need to keep a militant patriotism alive. That is what you will see in this section.

I AM GOYA

I am Goya
of the bare field, by the enemy's beak gouged
till the craters of my eyes gape
I am grief

I am the tongue
of war, the embers of cities
on the snows of the year 1941
I am hunger

I am the gullet
of a woman hanged whose body like a bell
tolled over a blank square
I am Goya

O grapes of wrath!
I have hurled westward
              the ashes of the uninvited guest!
and hammered stars into the unforgetting sky—like nails
I am Goya

ANDREI VOZNESENSKY, 1959
(Translated by Stanley Kunitz)

"WHY SHOULD WE
FIGHT WITH AMERICA?"

Mankind has now become mortal with the invention of weapons that could destroy all of us. People have come to understand this. Before a man is shot, he is supposed to see all his life in flashback. The existence of the hydrogen bomb is having that effect on mankind, including Russians.

> From an interview with a young Russian
> in Moscow in 1967 by British correspondent
> John Morgan, printed in *Encounter*, February, 1968

God, you see everything. God, God, God! Do something so that people no longer will kill each other on earth. God, do something so that there will remain only goodness and love in the world. Goodness and love!

> From a girl's prayer in a play about World
> War II, *The Night of the Nightingales*,
> by Valentin Yezhov, in the magazine *Teatr*
> (*Theater*), No. 1, 1969

Possibly one can forgive Inge for her naiveté in praying to God. But there is no excuse for a Soviet writer to take the position that all war is evil, to equate Pyotr [a Russian], whose father was killed at the beginning of the war, with Inge [a German], whose father was killed on the Eastern front.

> From the armed forces newspaper *Krasnaya
> zvezda (Red Star)*, April 13, 1969

There are more than enough races on the earth,
A whole palette of colors.
Everybody inhales two and a half liters
Of air at one time.
If this goes on, goodbye to everything,
We'll soon see the end of our era.
Those Chinese will in a few years
Deprive the earth of its atmosphere.
I have had the same dream day after day for a week,
A nightmare from which I awaken.
I dream that sitting in the kitchen
Are Mao Tse-tung and Syngman Rhee,
And our little globe has been divided
Into three enormous parts.
A billion of us and a billion of them and the rest are
  Chinese.
They hand me a sheet of paper of some kind,
Here, they say, sign it, go ahead!
We really need your Far East,
Oh how badly we need it.
I keep recalling this dream,
I keep thinking of it all the time.
I even addressed a salesgirl recently
As Mao, pardon me, Tse-tung.
But soon we will fly to the moon
And why should we fight with America!
The left part for them, the right for us
And the Chinese can have the rest.

From an unpublished song written before
1969 by the actor V. Vysotsky

THE DOVE AND THE OLIVE BRANCH, OR THE HAMMER AND SICKLE?

There is a revealing glimpse of different attitudes in the society toward East-West tensions and the possibility of war in the novel What Is It You Want? *by Vsevolod Kochetov, which appeared in the magazine* Oktiabr (October), *No. 9, 1969.*

"Tell me in all frankness, what do you think of today's young people?"

"It seems to me you already know."

"No, what I want are precise words and not general outlines. Precisely what you think and why." Felix pulled up a chair and sat down opposite his father.

"On the whole, everything seems to be in the right place," said Sergei Antropovich. "You people are educated; you know a few things about life; your minds are developed and sharp. When we were your age, many of us could hardly talk. Whereas you people have a lot of Ciceros among you. So everything's fine and at the same time it's disturbing—very disturbing."

"Why? How come?"

Sergei Antropovich shifted a pile of the latest newspapers

DOVE AND OLIVE BRANCH OR HAMMER AND SICKLE? § 203

that lay on his lap. "The world situation, my friend, is like a taut string—it hums with tension. They are waging such a campaign against us that it may even be worse than when those fourteen governments attacked the Soviet Republic in 1919."

"And what are you thinking? That if something happens we won't bear up, but will run away into the bushes?"

"That's not the point, not at all. Maybe some people will run—certainly they'll run—and others, I have no doubt, will go into battle with chest forward. The point is something else. That you people are carefree; you believe too much in the peace-loving sirens—both the ones abroad and ours here at home. Your emblem has become the Biblical dove with the olive branch in its beak. Whoever slipped it to you in place of the hammer and sickle?

"Father, I hope that when you say 'you people,' you don't mean me personally. Let's be clear about that."

"All right. Now look, you see these newspapers? Even though little is said about it and the print is small, practically every day lately there have been reports about a new fascist party in the Federal Republic of Germany, the so-called National-Democratic Party. This is a menacing danger. West Germany is full of nationalists. And you youngsters take everything lightly. Your efforts are all focused on pleasure, on enjoying yourselves—that is to say, on consumption. The passion for consumption! Of course, that is nice; it's pleasant. Have a good time. We didn't always have our noses to the grindstone, ourselves, you know. We weren't monks, either: look at how many of you youngsters we produced. But we were not carefree, Felix, I can tell you that. Day and night, on weekdays and holidays, we prepared for the fact that sooner or later they would attack us. We learned how to fight and to defend our government and our system, our present and your future."

A FOURTEEN-YEAR-OLD

IN SVERDLOVSK

The emphasis on developing patriotism in young people can be felt throughout the educational system, not only in courses on Russian history and Soviet Communism but in the broadest sense as well, through the study of literature and the arts. The spirit of this emphasis is well expressed in the opening paragraphs of an article in the magazine Selskaya molodezh *(Village Youth), No. 5, 1969.*

I recall that a fourteen-year-old lad who was a pupil in one of the Sverdlovsk schools said to me bitterly, "Loyalty to one patch of land is narrow-mindedness. It is a primitive feeling for one's own pasture. Why can't I love all places?"

"Of course you should love them," I said, "but to begin with you should understand that the homeland is not just a patch of land, a favorite landscape. It is a way of thinking, it is ideals and concepts of justice and duty—everything that is dear to you on earth."

He looked away and for a while we walked along in silence.

"Rousseau and Thoreau were also true to their ideals," he said cautiously.

"They loved their homeland."

"Do you mean to say that these men who advocated equality and a return to nature were nationalists?"

"No, they were great patriots."

Above, first-graders are brought to Red Square to place flowers at Lenin's tomb. Below, older children decorate one of the Soviet Union's many memorials to soldiers who died in World War II. *(Tass)*

FROM WAR LITERATURE

*Here are excerpts from two works of Soviet war
literature that aroused controversy in the press.
They stand out from the bulk of war writings
in that they bring to the understanding of the
war the creative artist's spirit of humanity. They
remind Soviet readers that whatever else it was,
World War II was mostly a time of grief and
loss, of hardship and suffering. The first piece is
a long story by Viktor Nekrasov called "The
Second Night," which appeared in the early
1960's. The second is a play, The Night of the
Nightingales, by Valentin Yezhov, which was
staged in Moscow at the end of the 1960's.*

*"The Second Night" is about an eighteen-
year-old village boy's introduction to the war.
At the beginning, Leonid Bogorad, known as
Lenka, and his comrades are making their way
to the front. On his second night at the front,
Lenka goes out on a scouting mission with Captain Orlik to look for enemy mines. While crawl-
ing through the grass holding his knife in his
teeth, he comes upon a German, a muscular German. Lenka struggles with him for a long time
and finally prevails. Exhausted, his shirt torn,
Lenka and his captain return to headquarters
where this scene takes place.*

"Come here. I'll show you a new acquaintance
of yours."

Lenka, still tucking in his shirt, went over to the table.

"Do you recognize him?" Orlik held out a photograph.

The small snapshot had uneven borders, as if it had been torn; it showed a bright-eyed, smiling boy with a turned-up nose and a lock of hair on his forehead, wearing a white shirt that was unbuttoned. Orlik threw two more snapshots on the table. On one of them was the same boy in just his bathing trunks, on the beach, sitting with his arms around his knees, and next to him a girl in a bathing suit and cap. The other photo showed an old man with a high collar and an elderly woman, and the same boy and girl: he wearing a jacket and tie, his hair painstakingly combed, without the forelock, and she in a light-colored dress with a flower in her hair.

Lenka raised his eyes to the captain, who, looking at him jovially, gathered up the snapshots and held them like a fan in his outstretched hand. "Johann-Amadei Hetzke. Senior Lance Corporal. Born in Mannheim in 1925. Killed on the Russian front in 1943 in the region of Golaya Dolina on the night of— What's the date today, Bogatkin?"

"The twenty-fifth," said the engineer.

"On the night of twenty-five July, killed by Soviet soldier Leonid Bogorad. Now, soldier, do you recognize him?"

Lenka didn't take his eyes from the picture; he kept looking at the cheerful, smiling, snub-nosed face. Out there in the field, by the pear trees bruised from shells, he had not seen that face. But the neck, that strong round neck— He turned away, he couldn't look at it.

"We don't live too badly, Bogorad. We have an international selection here—Hungarian cognac, Swiss chocolate, Portuguese sardines. Now confess, have you ever eaten sardines? You'll lick your fingers. Listen, tear yourself away from those photos. Been admiring the golden-haired Gretchen?"

Lenka silently gave him back the photographs.

"She's not bad, eh?" Orlik, squinting one eye, looked at the snapshot. "The dead boy had good taste in women, it looks to me."

Lenka looked sullenly at the captain and lowered his eyes. "Don't talk like that, Comrade Captain."

But the captain didn't hear, or acted as if he didn't hear. He went over to the table, took some glasses and held one out to Lenka. "Here's to your baptism in fire, Leonid Semyonovich! To your second night of combat."

Lenka stood there silently with his head down.

"On the first night you got acquainted with mines. And with us. And on the second night, with this here Hetzke. Say, why have you become gloomy? The captain took him by the chin. "Have a drink, it will cheer you up."

Lenka shook his head.

"What's the matter with you? Are you sick? Bogatkin, get a thermometer. Good God, he's fallen ill."

"Allow me to go, Comrade Captain," said Lenka very quietly.

"Where?" Orlik stood in front of Lenka, holding a shaving mug in one hand and a cut glass tumbler in the other, both full to the brim. "Where to?"

"Nowhere. I'll wait for you outside."

"But only this evening when we were going out on the job, you yourself—"

Lenka raised his head and looked the captain in the eye. "Allow me to go, Comrade Captain," he repeated insistently, but just as quietly.

The captain turned around sharply, went over to the table, put down the glasses, stood there a few seconds and then, not turning around, said, "Go." And when Lenka had gone, he drank a whole glass in one gulp.

Vtoraya noch, rasskazy (The Second Night, Stories), Moscow, 1965

*The war has just ended in Germany. A Soviet
occupation soldier, Pyotr, meets a German girl,
Inge, just at the time when, unknown to him,
an order is issued forbidding fraternization between Soviet military personnel and German ci-
vilians. Inge is a lonely and bitter girl who has
lost her entire family in the war. Pyotr gradually
wins her confidence and in a matter of hours the
two feel a growing attraction to one another.
They spend a night walking and talking and shyly
kissing each other, and toward morning they sit
down in the park and doze off, her head on his
shoulder. Lieutenant Fedorovsky finds them there
and proceeds to bring serious formal charges
against Pyotr, which are then challenged by two
other officers. It is this picture of dissention in the
ranks that makes the play unusual, and the fact
that a colonel is willing to flout military discipline
in order to save Pyotr from unjust punishment.
These excerpts begin at the point where the
young couple are discovered in the park and Inge,
frightened, jumps up and runs off.*

FEDOROVSKY: Halt! Stop immediately. Stop, girl, or I'll shoot!
(Takes out his pistol and raises it for a warning shot into
the air. PYOTR suddenly strides over, takes the hand hold-
ing the weapon, and pulls it down.)
PYOTR: There's no need to frighten her, Comrade Lieutenant.
FEDOROVSKY: Wha-a-t?!
PYOTR: Don't frighten her. She's frightened enough as it is.
FEDOROVSKY: (pulling his hand free) You've gone out of your
mind, Sergeant! Do you realize what you're doing?
PYOTR: I do.
FEDOROVSKY: So-o—(Gives PYOTR a quietly poisonous look.)
And now perhaps you'll tell me where your rifle is,
Comrade Sergeant? (PYOTR rushes over to the tree.)
FEDOROVSKY: Stop!

PYOTR: You've hidden it, Comrade Lieutenant.

FEDOROVSKY: (sneering) If I've hidden it, that's not so bad. But what if the enemy stole it while you've been dallying around here with this German tart? And maybe some uncaptured fascists are already using it to shoot at our Soviet soldiers.

PYOTR: I beg you—I'm guilty of course, but I beg you not to talk that way about this girl. She's not a tart.

FEDOROVSKY: Well, who is she, then? Maybe she's your schoolmate with whom you made a date for six o'clock in the evening after the war? Cut out the fairytale stuff. How much did you give her? A loaf of bread and a tin of food? The girl looks pretty good—it was worth it!

PYOTR: (in a ringing whisper) If you weren't wearing the uniform of our army—

FEDOROVSKY: (mockingly) What then?

PYOTR: (unable to restrain himself any longer, strides over to the lieutenant, grabs him at the chest by the shirt and pulls the lieutenant toward him) I would simply punch you in the face! (Thrusts him aside with disgust.)

(Out of the bushes come Sergeant-Major KUZOVKOV, Sergeants ZUBOV and FIRSOV, and Private BUTENKO. FEDOROVSKY, in a fury, reaches for his holster, then restrains himself.)

FEDOROVSKY: All right, Sergeant. I treat you like one of us, and you, it turns out—you're a stubborn one. Okay, if that's how it is, I'll let you have it. I'll see to it that you regret this day for the rest of your life. I'll fix your biography.

[In a later scene, Fedorovsky reports the incident to his superior, First Lieutenant Timofeyev.]

FEDOROVSKY: I wrote down everything for you just as it happened.

TIMOFEYEV: And what did happen? You're accusing this boy of very serious political crimes.

FEDOROVSKY: In your opinion, to strike an officer in the face is not a political crime?

TIMOFEYEV: In a certain sense, yes. And he should be punished for that by a certain procedure. But you, in giving me your report, with this wording of yours, you're sending him straight to a court martial. By the way, Lieutenant, aren't you being struck in the face too often these days?

FEDOROVSKY: Comrade First Lieutenant!

TIMOFEYEV: All right, I'm sorry. Now, let's see. This boy insulted you personally and you are accusing him of state crimes, of betraying the homeland, of ties with the enemy, and so forth. (FEDOROVSKY is silent. His face is turned away.) Do you understand what would happen if everyone who is insulted personally portrayed his offender as a state criminal?

[Timofeyev has doubts about Fedorovsky's version of what happened and decides to look into the matter himself. But by this time news of the incident has reached a higher level, and Timofeyev gets a telephone call from his commander ordering him to send all the evidence and reports about the case to the procurator's office. He puts the receiver down and turns to Fedorovsky.]

TIMOFEYEV: Why did you destroy the boy, Lieutenant?

FEDOROVSKY: Excuse me, Comrade First Lieutenant, I don't understand you. What do you mean "destroy"? I reported everything just as it was.

TIMOFEYEV: How was it?

FEDEROVSKY: Very simple. How he rolled around with her in the park under the oak tree, how—

TIMOFEYEV: There are no oak trees there; there are maples.

FEDOROVSKY: What?

TIMOFEYEV: There are no oak trees in the park—they're maples.

FEDOROVSKY: What's the difference? Oaks, maples—what does it matter?

TIMOFEYEV: When it concerns a person, it matters a great deal. Oaks or maples, he sat or he lay, or he rolled around, as you put it. Ah, Lieutenant, Lieutenant. Why have you destroyed the boy?

[Timofeyev's superior, Colonel Lukyanov, quickly takes steps to free Pyotr by adding his name to a list of soldiers who are being demobilized and are leaving for home the next morning. He knows he is jeopardizing his own career by disobeying the commander's orders, yet he says that he must do this not only for Pyotr's sake but for his own as well.]

LUKYANOV: It is very easy to say nothing can be done to help this man, and then let the matter drop. You let it drop once and then a second time, and then nothing is left that is sacred. And one cannot live without something sacred. One cannot.

Teatr (Theater), No. 1, 1969

WHAT THE MILITARY MEN SAY

The Soviet military leaders have been very critical of stories, plays, and movies that focus on the tragic, inhuman side of war. They say that soul-searching and subtleties in literature are no help to them in training good young soldiers; what the military want is an uncomplicated and fairly primitive war literature. Over the years, there has been a continuous battle between them and the more independent and gifted Soviet writers, and the real question has been whether the military would be allowed to stand in the way of a more humanistic and sensitive approach to the war and would insist on social engineering from the writers. Here are some comments that are typical of what military men have been saying.

Lieutenant General N. Demin, 1964:

Sometimes faint notes of an abstract condemnation of war, the demand to turn weapons into scrap, and appeals against war in general steal into the works of some young writers and artists who have not completed the strict school of warfare or army training. It is necessary to indoctrinate in young people love of and respect for the army and its weapons and to speak out with all our might against feelings of dejection, fear, and depression.

The youth who enter the army now are an excellent rein-
forcement; they are literate and cultured. But they do not
have enough everyday experience, and they have not seen
the burdens and suffering of war. Writers and artists, our
creative workers, must fill this gap in life experience.

Prostor (Scope), No. 9, 1964

Marshal Rodion Ya. Malinovsky, 1964:

One cannot fail to call attention to the fact that in recent
times mistaken tendencies in representing the last war have
appeared. Motifs of pacifism and the abstract rejection of
war have made themselves felt in certain works of literature
and painting and in movies. Is it correct to represent the war
our people waged as merely an accumulation of horrors and
deprivations, to trot out onto the stage in naturalistic detail
little, confused people? We reject this one-sided approach to
an important theme.

Yes, war is cruel, inhuman, and destructive. But after all,
the sacrifices that fell to our lot are filled with a most profound meaning, they were made for the sake of the people
and their freedom.

Neither can we ignore certain views that have appeared,
particularly in critical literature, calling for a rejection of
enthusiastic words, of the heroic aspect in works about the
war, and claiming, if you please, that all this used to be a
feature of the period of the cult of the personality. We are
against hollow, pompous works but, faithful to truth, we
cannot engage in playing down the heroism of our people.

Krasnaya zvezda (Red Star), February 9, 1964

Marshal I. S. Konev, 1969:

Great harm is done to the upbringing of young people by
the fact that recently some writers have set about the revision
of heroes on whom more than one generation of Soviet

young people has been reared. Doubts are sometimes even cast on the exploits of the Panfilovites, Zoya Kosmodemyanskaya, the Young Guards, and others.

It is especially important for literature to depict the image of our contemporary fighting man. Despite a certain increase in literature about the army of our time, the creative task in this sphere remains urgent.

Krasnaya zvezda, March 27, 1969

A live-statue tableau on the twenty-fifth anniversary of the founding of the wartime underground organization of the Komsomol   *(Tass)*

THE WHOLE TRUTH

Konstantin Simonov has written some of the most widely read popular novels about World War II (among them, Days and Nights *and* The Living and the Dead, *both available in English). At the Soviet Writers' Congress in May, 1967, he said it is important, while remaining responsive to the needs of the military in literature, not to conceal or underplay the harsh sides of war in the training of young soldiers. The following excerpt from that speech is from the May 31, 1967, issue of* Literaturnaya gazeta *(Literary Gazette).*

If we writers do not speak the whole truth about the past, we will never win the complete trust of the young people reading our books.

To illustrate my words with just one example, having written unequivocally that the responsibility for the gravity of our situation in 1941, which brought the fascists to the walls of Moscow, lies primarily on the shoulders of Stalin, one must also say another thing: that his speech in Red Square on November 7, 1941, played a very important role in saving Moscow from surrender to the fascists.

We Soviet writers are the most confirmed allies of peace and fighters for peace. But once a military danger exists, and an army exists that defends the peaceful achievements of

Winners in one of the troop-landing competitions at the
"Zarnitsa" military sports games   (*Tass*)

socialism, there exists a problem for us writers of educating
young soldiers through literature. I think a well-trained
soldier is one who knows that war is a difficult thing, in
particular, he knows this from material about the last war,
and is prepared for difficulty. But the soldier whom literature
and movies do not tell what war actually is, and in particular
do not tell how the last war was, is a poorly trained soldier
in the moral sense, because if he has to face war, in spite of
all our efforts in the struggle for peace, its gravity will be
more unexpected for him than for the soldier who is educated on truthful literature about the war.

LOW-KEYED LOYALTY

Nowhere is the generation gap more acutely evident than in discussions about World War II, as you will see from these two pieces. The first is from a Moscow high school student's composition. The second is by Viktor Nekrasov, author of The Second Night, *who fought in the Battle of Stalingrad and wrote perhaps the most famous book on it,* In the Trenches of Stalingrad. *In this story, "The Incident on Mamai Hill," he describes a return visit to Stalingrad, by boat down the Volga, and an encounter he has with two young soldiers for whom present-day events hold far more interest than memorials to the past. In both these excerpts, the youngsters express confidence that if the need arose, they would fight for their country as courageously as their fathers and grandfathers did. This low-keyed, undemonstrative loyalty, which doesn't require constant public reaffirmation, seems to me to be characteristic of how very many young people feel.*

Before this, I had read a great deal about the war, but I imagined it to be completely different. Simonov's book changed my attitude in many ways toward that terrible grief through which the whole nation, the whole land, lived while repelling the barbaric attack of the fascists. I have often heard it said by people of the generation that lived through the Revolution and then through the war that modern youth does not value and cannot evaluate the great feat our fathers performed. In my opinion, this is not true. It is simply a prejudice. I do not doubt that we, too, are capable of such feats.

Literatura v shkole (Literature in the School), No. 5, 1964

They turned out to be good lads. Both from the Volga region, both towheads with crew cuts, and smart-looking in their uniforms with white undercollars. They had just finished their military service and were going home, and they were very shy and kept straightening the folds of their shirts. So I did the talking. And naturally I talked about the war—about Stalingrad.

To this day, I blush at the memory of that evening. I talked without stopping. I recalled various episodes and comrades, I explained what the situation was, I drew some diagrams, but the main thing I did was talk. The boys discreetly ate sausage and listened to me very attentively without interrupting, but I think that more than anything else they wanted to go to sleep. Yet I went on talking and talking—I tried to convince them of a few things and argued about others, and once in a while I would pause to reflect and then utter a significant "Ah, yes."

When the boys left—and they somehow did it all of a sudden, getting up and saying. "It's time for us to go. Thank you very much."—I suddenly felt ashamed, especially because I had so persistently and repeatedly invited them to accompany me to Mamai Hill. "I was a regimental engineer there; I know everything about the place." They looked at each other and thanked me, then stood up and said it was time to go.

When the boat docked in Stalingrad at dawn the next morning, Nekrasov went along to Mamai Hill. He searched for and found, in the basement

of a meat-processing plant, the dugout room that
had served as headquarters for his regiment dur-
ing the days of heavy fighting. As he approached
it along a dark corridor, he saw cases of unused
cartridges that had been sitting there for twenty-
three years. The past began to flood in on him,
and by the time he pushed open the familiar iron
door to the dugout, a moment later, he was
totally immersed in the world of November, 1942.
He spent that day reliving the Battle of Stalin-
grad, both as it actually happened and as his writ-
er's imagination had reshaped it in the years since.
Toward nightfall he returned to the boat.

In the evening of the same day, as I was coming out of my
cabin, I bumped right into my soldier-lads. They greeted me
politely and walked past; then the older of the two turned
back to me. "Excuse me, but we would like it very much if
you would—Maybe you'll accept our invitation?"

There was no free table in the restaurant, so we had to
take one that had an elderly bald man sitting mournfully in
front of some sturgeon and a half-empty decanter of what
looked like port. "Do you mind if we join you?" asked the
older lad.

"Well, as long as you're here, sit down."

After our first drink and a toast to the hero-city we had just
left, the younger soldier made another effort to start the conversation—it somehow just wouldn't get started—by asking
me, "Where did you scratch your hands so badly?"

I looked at my hands and they really were scratched up.
"On Mamai Hill," I said.

"You went up there?"

"Yes."

"And did you see the Shah of Iran?"

"No."

"We saw him."

"And how was he?"

"Not bad. He's impressive looking, with gray hair and dark glasses. They say he's forty-six. And his wife was with him— she's the dark-eyed type."

"An architect by training," our neighbor put in with a gloomy voice.

"That's right, she's an architect," the younger soldier readily agreed. "They say she studied in Paris."

For some time the conversation turned on the subject of the Shah and his wife, his retinue and the limousines, the wreaths of flowers and the honor guard. Then it began to lapse. The soldiers felt awkward and I was silent, but our despondent neighbor, who had ordered another decanter of wine for himself, began to perk up. "I look at you young fellows—defenders of the Homeland—and you know what I'm thinking? Did you go see the site of the great battles, the great bloodletting, where men gave their lives so that things would be good for you? Not for their generation, but yours. No, all you saw was the Shah of Iran and his wife. So a Shah comes, so what? He lays a wreath and they all lay wreaths, and you fellows stand there gaping."

"Well, it was the first time for us, and, after all, it's interesting," the soldiers replied timidly.

"What's so interesting? To look at a czar? I also did some fighting up on the hill, as things worked out. Not on Mamai Hill itself, but I did go there on occasion. You wouldn't know the place now. It's not the hill any more, but a symbol. A symbol of your fathers and their heroism."

At once the boys took offense. "Don't lecture us," said the older one. "We know as well as anybody else what took place here. And if it ever comes down to that again, we ourselves would—" He broke off and, evidently embarrassed by the sharpness of his own words, offered his neighbor a Kazbek cigarette.

"No, thanks, I don't smoke. Haven't smoked for a long

time, for over a year. I wake up in the morning and don't even cough once. You don't believe it?" He looked at me. "Try it for yourself. You, I notice, smoke all the time. It's a pity, absolutely a pity. You're not a young man; you read books and newspapers; you obviously know about the ruinous effects of nicotine."

"And vodka too," I added. I looked at my lads. They could hardly keep from laughing. "What do you say we do a repeat of last night and go to my cabin," I said.

We went to my cabin. I did no more talking about the war. We just drank a reasonable amount of vodka and then said goodnight. With the remains of the vodka I made a compress for myself: The scratches on my hands had swollen and turned purple.

Novy mir (*New World*), No. 12, 1965.

THEY LOVED LEMONADE

*For those Soviet soldiers who were at Damansky
Island on the border with China in January, 1969,
the time to fight had come. After their encounter
with the Chinese was publicized, the Soviet press
wrote widely about the men of Damansky and
their heroism. The main theme was that while
the young people had had a fairly easy time of it
up until then, they were now beginning to get
their share of difficulties in life and were proving
that they could cope with them, just as their
elders had in their time. This is part of an article in* Smena (Generation), *No. 10, 1969, a
Komsomol magazine with a circulation of nearly
2 million.*

We talk out loud about the Revolution, industrialization, the Great Patriotic War, the reconstruction, the Virgin
Lands. And we think to ourselves about the Komsomol workers of Perekop and Kakhovka and Dneprostroi and Magnitka,
about the young heroes of Stalingrad and Berlin, and those
who conquered the steppes of Kazakhstan and worked as
experts on the new construction projects in Siberia. Each one
of these generations had its difficulties. Each one added its
decoration of honor to the red banner of the Komsomol.

And now it is the turn of those who were born a few
years after the victorious year 1945. The time of those for
whom not only the first five year plans and the war but even

the opening up of the Virgin Lands is history. When the first furrows were made in the ground of Kazakhstan and the Altai region, today's twenty-year-olds were toddling under the table.

Their life has been far easier than that of their predecessors. One must confess that their older brothers and fathers and grandfathers, who won this good life at the cost of blood and sweat, have sometimes fallen to reproaching the young: You people are not what we used to be. And it is hard to tell what there is more of in their words, envy of someone else's happiness or concern for the future of the new generation.

Of course, the young people could counter some of the reproaches with convincing arguments: If the sons are exact copies of the fathers and repeat their work—if they dream the same dreams—mankind will stop developing. The young people must go farther.

As for overcoming difficulties, the young had nothing to answer.

Damansky has answered for them, and 1969 has its twenty-year-old Pavel Korchagins and Alexander Matrosovs [the first is a literary hero of the Civil War and the second a real-life hero of World War II].

I tried to make a very simple study of the lives of these heroes of 1969. I looked at the biographical data on the rank-and-file soldiers and the sergeants, those who are not in the regular border guards by profession. Although I tried, I could detect no regular common patterns in their lives. Some had already worked as tractor drivers, truck drivers, and metal workers, but most of them came to the army directly from school. The only thing they had in common was the absence of any major event in their lives. Now their biographies have another thing in common: the defense of Damansky.

I also wanted to ask them what they wished to do in life. Those still alive named several professions. The dead— Well, how can you ask a dead man about this? Ten years later and fifty years later, he will still be a twenty-year-old rank-and-file hero of Damansky Island.

They showed me the Komsomol membership card, pierced by shrapnel and covered with blood, of Sergeant Boris Golovin. In the fighting he proved to be a courageous lad, and his comrades told me that in life he was a good friend, warm and exacting, a lad of justice and principle. He dreamed of studying in an institute after his military service. His notebook was filled with formulas of some kind, and he took it into battle with him. In his pocket they found fragments of a certificate for the badge of "Soldier-Sportsman" and a handwritten note, all bloodied and torn by a shell fragment. Boris had decided to hold a contest at his frontier post for sports lovers, and he had written down six questions about the national soccer tournament. The prize for the winner was to have been five bottles of lemonade, five cans of condensed milk, and three kilograms of honeycakes.

They loved lemonade and cakes; they were still boys. But at the hour of death, with no hesitation, they gave what is most precious of all to man.

PART EIGHT

Officially Sponsored Criticism and Voices of Dissent

The world over, young people are asking critical and fundamental questions about the systems under which they live. Is this also true in the Soviet Union? It is hard to find the answer by reading official Soviet sources. There is some discussion and criticism in the Soviet press, but as you will see it is limited in scope. To consider the matter more realistically, you have to look at the criticism that is not officially permitted—the underground letters, poems, songs, essays, documents, and other materials that circulate in handwritten or typewritten form. This section illustrates the range of criticism in Russia from that which limits itself to bureaucratic shortcomings all the way to that which challenges the basic principles of the system and is done in defiance of authority.

Officially Sponsored Criticism

Much of the within-system complaining by the young falls under two general headings—the performance of the economy and the quality of cultural life. The pieces in this first section of Part Eight deal with those two subjects.

ON CATCHING UP

WITH THE CAPITALISTS

A letter to Komsomolskaya pravda *on February 8, 1968, expressed vividly the sense of frustration that many young people feel about shortages of consumer goods and their irritation with the familiar slogans that are intended to reassure people.*

I am twenty-five years old. There are many questions about life that interest me and about which I would like to get advice. For example, in conversations at work and at home you hear people say that in other countries there is a lot of everything—cars, clothes, food—while here there is a shortage of this and a shortage of that. You meet a friend who has returned from abroad, and he is wearing a new suit that he got over there. In general, there is a lot of talk about foreign clothes.

On the other hand, you are told over and over again that "things are going well here," that we will "catch up with and overtake" the capitalists. Well, are we catching up? With whom? In what? In our country everybody talks in general terms, and you too will reply to my letter in general terms, won't you? I like precision. Give me facts.—V. S., engineer, Kharkov.

> A letter like the above is always published together with a reply or comment that corrects the negative impression it gives. In this case the companion piece was a review of a new statistical handbook published in Moscow entitled We and the Planet, in which Soviet output and development were favorably compared with those of other countries.

WHO IS TO BLAME?

*The Soviet press is full of complaints about in-
efficiency and bad planning, red tape, bungling,
and graft in the economy. The regime encourages
such criticism as a way to keep officials on their
toes and to spur people on to more efficient production. From the stream of letters that come in
every day, the editors select some for follow-up
investigation by their correspondents. In this instance, Anatoly Agranovsky, writing for the leading government newspaper* Izvestia, *reports on a
letter from some young workers in Bratsk in
Siberia which led him to investigate the colossal
mismanagement in the building of a new aluminum factory out there. Here is the first part of
his article, which appeared on February 11, 1967.*

The pipe was laid by Luzgin's brigade, in which there
were Komsomol volunteers, demobilized soldiers, local people, recruited workers, and even one fellow who was "out
early on probation": They had released him before the end
of his term—what he was in prison for, he didn't like to say.
But he worked well, as did everyone, for the brigade did not
tolerate shirkers. Luzgin himself was a sullen Siberian, about
thirty years old, lean and bearded. He grew his beard after
Fidel Castro visited Bratsk [in 1964]: At that time many
people grew beards. Luzgin was not too bright, but he knew
his job and the men obeyed him.

They worked in the tunnel. Like the *burlaki* [peasants
who towed the barges in old Russia], they hauled a kilometer-

long cable and wound it around sections of steel piping
weighing up to 880 pounds, which were then, with a terrible
scraping noise and sparks flying over the concrete floor,
dragged by a power winch into the gloomy depths. There
the mechanization came to an end; there was no room for it.
"Work with the crowbar!" "Once again, easier now." "Your
hands! Watch out for your hands!" "Ready now—let's go!"
"Now—weld." They knew the job was urgent; they worked
well together; the work was going smoothly, and because of
that the brigade was in a good mood and things went even
better.

By the end of the third week they had finished most of
the laying job. Resting on metal supports, several lines of
straight, clean pipes stretched under the ground, and it was a
sight that gladdened the eye, as does any work done well.
But then the section chief told the brigade leader that the
337- and 89-millimeter pipe had to be cut up into pieces and
discarded.

"Why?" Luzgin asked.

"We're going to substitute another size."

"I see," said Luzgin, and the muscles under his cheekbones
began to work. "Why didn't they think of that sooner?"

"It was a mistake made by the design people. Tell the boys
it won't affect their wages."

They sent Kasha Burdukov, a first-class acetylene torch
cutter, to do the cutting job. He is a silent type and did not
curse. He turned around and went off, but as they told me
later, "the expression on his face was really something!" And
they all went into the tunnel as if to a funeral. There was
nothing to the cutting: Kasha opened the valves, adjusted
the flame, stepped back a bit from the seam, and with one
quick motion undid the work that had been done.

If at least six months had gone by, they could have explained to themselves (or accepted an explanation) that this
alteration was necessary and beneficial. But as it was, nobody

even tried to explain anything to them. A new order had simply been issued and they had to carry it out, as Luzgin put it, without any talk.

But talk about it could not be avoided, and in the end a letter was sent to *Izvestia*.

"Dear Editor! We are the builders of BRAZ—the Bratsk Aluminum Factory. It is one of the giants of the five-year plan, and we are doing everything we can to build it well and finish on schedule. But we are being hindered by the bunglers who are designing the factory.

"Take, for example, the latest case involving A. Luzgin's brigade. The work of ten men over twenty days was wasted, and so were 340 linear meters of steel pipe. And with a shortage of labor and materials at BRAZ! Who allowed this to happen? The answer as always was incomprehensible: 'the fault of the planning organization.'

"We workers are not satisfied with such explanations. There is nothing more insulting than having to do over your own work and not even knowing who is to blame. Has anybody considered what this does to people's morale? Some say that there is no reason to make a fuss since the brigade is being paid for all the work. Paid for assembling and for dismantling too. But man lives not by bread alone. We are conscientious workers and our labor must always be conscientious.

"What do we propose? We want the guilty person to be found and sent out here so we can have a look at him and he can look at his handiwork. It doesn't matter if he is away from his office for a week. There will be less wastage on the building site, and he will learn a few things when he talks with the workers and really assesses his mistake.

"We ask *Izvestia* to verify all the facts and find out who is to blame for our situation."

It was this assignment from the readers that brought me to Bratsk.

SVETLANA'S CULTURAL PITCH

A factory mechanic writing in Komsomolskaya pravda *on June 3, 1967, criticized the cultural propaganda work in his factory for failing to reach and engage the young workers at their own cultural level.*

I would like to share some reflections occasioned by a visit I made to a class of the Outlook Political Circle at the Likhachev Plant [an automotive plant in Moscow]. The circle is led by Svetlana Lentsner, an engineer, a person of wide erudition and good taste; she is considered one of the best propagandists at the plant. That day Svetlana was giving a lecture on aesthetic upbringing. The lecture was meaningful and interesting, but for some reason the five seventeen- and eighteen-year-olds at the lecture were openly yawning.

Later, after talking with the youngsters, I realized why the lecture had been a chore for them. Svetlana spoke of the fascination of ballroom dancing, but they are happy dancing the shake and the twist, and they turn off the television if a ballet is on. She spoke emotionally about the enjoyment to be derived from a meaningful motion picture and the insignificance of mere popular hits, whereas her listeners had seen *The Magnificent Seven* three or four times each. Svetlana has complained that she has no desire to work with them because nothing interests them.

But after all, this is not the case: If someone is unexcited by what excites me, can it really be asserted that nothing at all excites him? The interests of the members of the circle are primitive and narrow, but they exist and, alas, it is precisely those interests that the youngsters are trying to pursue. Svetlana's more exalted interests arouse in them neither curiosity nor envy. The life experience of these boys is insignificant, but again, it cannot be said to be nonexistent.

A person obviously devises his "personal philosophy" depending on what he wants, depending on his personal interests—and in order to protect these interests. Here is the philosophizing of the youngsters in Outlook: "Why torture myself by studying, when my grandfather didn't finish even two grades, and look how well he lives"; "I want to get into a construction battalion in the army: when I come back I'll have money and I'll get some smart clothes."

After becoming better acquainted with the youngsters in Svetlana Lentsner's circle, I realized that they were not at all inclined to consider their interests immoral and that these interests were by no means tormenting the boys' consciences. The youngsters do not yet realize what these interests entail for them in the future; for the present they see their interests as truly human.

I remember a case from my career. I used to work together with two fellows and a girl at this same Likhachev plant. They too were between seventeen and nineteen, and the level of their interests differed little from that of Svetlana Lentsner's charges. All my attempts to fascinate these youngsters with my favorite books and to bring them into contact with something aesthetic had no success. But one day, completely by accident, we began to argue about *War and Peace*. And then, not expecting them to understand me, but more for myself, I began to discuss what Andrei Bolkonsky felt after he had met Natasha. I talked for a long time and suddenly sensed that they were listening to me with interest. The next day they sat down next to me and said in unison:

"Well, come on."

"Come on what?"

"Talk about something like what you talked about yester-day."

I think it is something as elementary as this that Svetlana needs in order really to fascinate her listeners. She obviously never stopped to consider why matters that are interesting and essential to her leave the youngsters totally indifferent; she has lost sight of the most important thing: Her listeners do not possess the intellectual level on which she was attempting to dance, so to speak.

In short, we are convinced once again that it is difficult to be a propagandist.

"THANK YOU,

COMRADE PROFESSOR"

Another way of handling the theme of young workers and cultural propaganda is through satirical stories or short features called feuilletons. This story appeared in Literaturnaya gazeta *(Literary Gazette), No. 31, 1969.*

In our factory they recently scheduled a lecture about Derzhavin. Gavriil Romanovich. The nineteenth-century poet. Well, you know, about how he had already spotted talent in the young Pushkin and before dying had given him his blessing. [Derzhavin died in 1816, when Pushkin was 17.]

When the shift was over we all stayed on; we gathered in the "red corner" [a place put aside for Party reading materials and conferences] and waited. The first one to speak was the chairman of our factory trade union committee, Chibirev. He introduced the lecturer, a professor who is a specialist in literature. Then a likable little old man of a professor went up to the rostrum and started to tell us about the poet Derzhavin. I must say, he was extremely interesting. About how Derzhavin was born in 1743, how he grew up, how his outlook on the world was formed, how he wrote odes, and mention of his relationship with Catherine the Great.

Then the professor recited some of Derzhavin's poems from memory. In short, it was a fascinating lecture. We listened and didn't even notice that two hours had flown by.

Finally, the professor finishes and sits down. The chairman of the factory committee, Chibirev, gets up and says, "Dear comrades, permit me in the name of everyone to thank the honored professor for an interesting lecture."

We applaud. The professor bows and says, "Thank you, comrades. Perhaps one of you has a question?"

Chibirev says, "Yes, comrades, if anyone wants to ask about something, don't be shy."

We are silent, thinking. Then the foreman of shop number two, Samsonov, gets up and says, "Here is my question: When will they finally get around to opening a cafeteria in our factory?"

The professor is taken aback. Chibirev is so startled that he winces, and says, "What's the matter with you, Samsonov? What are you asking about? That's an immaterial question!"

"How is it immaterial?" says Samsonov. "For over three months now the factory committee has been promising us a cafeteria, and it keeps dragging on. And meanwhile we have to dash five blocks to get something to eat at lunch break; we waste a lot of time. We have no time to read Derzhavin!"

Chibirev is all worked up and shouts, "Sit down, Samsonov. You're embarrassing us in front of the professor!" And now, addressing everyone, "Comrades, please ask questions that are to the point, that relate directly to the poet Derzhavin!"

Again we sit and are silent. Samsonov raises his hand again.

Chibirev asks suspiciously, "Samsonov, is your question about Derzhavin?"

"Yes, it is," says Samsonov.

"All right, then ask it!" says Chibirev.

Samsonov gets up and says, "I would like to know how the

Workers in Bratsk   (*Novosti*)

poet Derzhavin arranged his working day? What was his lunch break like? Was there a cafeteria right nearby or did he have to ride the bus for twenty minutes to get to one?"

Chibirev turns purple with rage and he screams, "Are you trying to make fools of us, Samsonov? How could there have been any buses two hundred years ago?"

"Well, if there were no buses," says Samsonov, "I am sure that the poet Derzhavin thought out this question and that he got a tasty meal quickly and not far from where he worked and this contributed to high productivity in his work!"

At this point the professor gets up and says, "Comrade Samsonov is absolutely right. The poet Derzhavin was not a gourmet, but he very much respected his mealtimes and he liked to sit down at a nicely set table. Here for example is how he described it in the poem 'Life in Zvanka':

'The ham is crimson, the sorrel soup with yolk of egg is
    green,
The meat pie is a ruddy yellow, the cheese is pale, the
    crayfish are red,
The caviar is like tar-black amber and with a blue plume
The pike is motley-colored—marvelous!' "

"Thank you, Comrade Professor, for supporting me!" says Samsonov. "Comrade Chibirev, I think that, after this poetry, to delay any further on a cafeteria in our factory is just plain disrespect to the memory of the famous Russian poet, Derzhavin!"

Now Chibirev is put out and says, "That's enough, Samsonov. We've got the idea. Tomorrow, in the factory committee, we'll settle this question of the cafeteria! There's no point in mixing Derzhavin up in all this. Are there no more questions?"

"No," says Samsonov. "Everything's clear."

With this, the lecture comes to an end. We all disperse feeling very satisfied.

And Samsonov says, "You see what it means to link poetry with life at the right moment. You see the effect you get! They say that next week we'll have a lecture by another professor about the poet Tiutchev. I'll use him to raise the question of a day-care nursery for the factory."

THE TATTOOED POEM

A direct assault on party censorship in the arts is impermissible in the Soviet press. Yet a good deal can be said by reducing the whole subject to the level of the ridiculous, as this writer has done. The story appeared in Yunost (Youth), *No. 1, 1965.*

I went into the editor's office. "Hello," I said.

"Hello," he growled.

"I brought a poem," I said timidly.

"Give it to the secretary."

"Can't do that. I have to go to work tomorrow."

"What's that got to do with it? Leave the manuscript and go on to work."

"Well, you see, I'm it. The manuscript is me."

"You!"

"Yes. Since we're supposed to economize on paper, I've taken to writing verse on myself. I tattoo it on."

"So what is it you want?"

"I'd like you to look at it and if possible print it in your magazine."

"Undress," said the editor, and rolled up his sleeves. I undressed. The editor read me over several times. "Not a bad poem," he said, "but it can't appear in the magazine like that."

"Naturally," I agreed. "You can't publish a nude photograph. You have to print it the usual way."

THE TATTOOED POEM §241

"That isn't what I meant. I don't mean the form, I mean the content. I don't like those two lines on your stomach, they'll have to be cut."

"But that's the best part of the whole thing. It'll be sure to hurt."

"Do you think it did not hurt Gogol to burn the second part of *Dead Souls*?"

"But Gogol burned paper, and I would have to cut my own flesh. And in one of the most sensitive places of all!"

"Don't worry," said the editor, "you are in good hands." And he grabbed a scalpel. After a minor operation my lines of poetry had been replaced by a few scars. "There, that's better," said the editor as he reread me. "Did that hurt?"

"Yes, it did," I admitted.

"That's only because you are not used to it. After a while you will be able to operate on yourself as well as I can."

"Is that all?"

"As far as I'm concerned. Go see the senior editor."

The senior editor sat behind a large table covered with a white sheet. "Lie down," he said. I lay down. He made his diagnosis: "Everything on the left leg has to go."

"Then what will I do with the right leg?" I objected.

"To tell the truth, young man, I don't like the right leg so much either. But we can fix the whole thing if we just change the ending as follows." The senior editor started sticking me rapidly with a needle. I writhed in pain.

"What you are doing is awful!" I shouted. "I don't want an end like that."

"Take it easy, it won't kill you."

"Hurry up with the period!" I pleaded.

The senior editor thought about it. "No, I believe dots would do better here," he said and plunged the needle three more times.

"Well, how is it going? Better?" he asked when I came to.

"No, worse," I sighed.

"Pull yourself together, young man. You must go in to see the editor-in-chief now."

"But I can't walk." They took me to the editor-in-chief on a stretcher. He stood in the middle of a big bright room; he wore a white smock and rubber gloves. The secretary next to him was also in white. They put me down. I could hear the orders: "Scalpel! Clamps! Camphor!"

Then I lost consciousness.

Two weeks later I was discharged from the editorial offices. I was pale and had lost weight. The editor shook my bandaged hand, slapped my wounded shoulder, and said: "You're pretty weak as a poet. You did not hold out. My advice to you is, next time write it down on paper. Paper can stand anything."

Translation by Atlas magazine

A KIND OF ALIENATION

Whether the leadership can evoke constructive responses from the new generation is a question. Viktor Rozov, a playwright who has written about young people, made a relevant observation in Literaturnaya gazeta, (Literary Gazette), No. 27, 1969.

A completely new generation is now coming in to take the place of those who were young just a short while ago, literally, six or seven years ago.

There is one feature inherent in some of these sixteen- and seventeen-year-olds that troubles me. It is their peculiar kind of alienation (of course, I am basing this on personal observation and not on generalized investigations). We adults co-exist with them in the same space and time, but we don't get through to each other. You say things to your son or daughter. The boys and girls of six to seven years ago—it used to happen—would shout back passionately, "You're wrong, your ideas are rigid, you are ancient." Today's youngsters don't shout and argue. They listen to what you say, then go ahead and do what they themselves think should be done, even when they are on good terms with their parents.

How do I explain this alienation? Evidently there is something extremely important that we have not given our children, and there are areas where we don't understand one another. As a result, they have developed a kind of self-defense around their own world of feelings.

Voices of Dissent

The material in the second part of this chapter has not been published in the Soviet press. With the exception of the first item, which is a song, it belongs to samizdat, the "publish-it-yourself" underground writing that circulates in carbon copies from hand to hand, and sometimes reaches the outside world. No collection of voices from Russia could pretend to be complete without dealing with the writing that does not appear in the Soviet press. Soviet officials are very sensitive about material such as this, though they themselves are not inattentive to voices of dissent in other countries.

ASK, BOYS!

In one of his "underground" songs, Alexander Galich urges young people to go on questioning their parents about the mistakes of the Stalin period. How and why did things go wrong? This is still a painful subject, especially for Russians over forty, and many would prefer to forget—if their offspring would only let them.

The boy asks: Why?
The boy asks: Why?
Two hundred and three hundred times, "why,"
A small cloud crosses his brow.
But Papa is cutting his ham,
Papa is cutting his ham,
He chomps and cuts his ham
And does not answer.

Before him looms once again the past, the pain,
Once again boys are straining to get into the dust of battle,
Don't you frighten them and scare them away.
Go on asking, boys, go on asking!
Keep right on asking, boys, just ask!
Ask, and ask!

Ask, how and why.
Ask, how and why.
How and why and for what reason.
Ask your fathers, boys!
No matter how much they cut their ham,
No matter how much they cut their ham,
No matter how much they go on cutting.
In the end they just have to answer!

Suddenly the eye's pupil turns muddy,
And the old house slippers are pinching!
Don't you take pity on them, wear them out,
Keep asking, boys, keep asking,
　Ask!

FEELING ISOLATED

As the decade of the 1960's came to an end, the mood of one thoughtful young man in Moscow was pessimistic about the prospects for an early enlargement of political freedom in Russia. He expressed his thoughts in a conversation.

If there was isolation between Russia and the West before the Revolution, we have increased it five times since then. This is what I feel in my most discouraged moments. Not only are there no signs of real individualism developing here, but there is not even any talk about it. Talk is considered already a kind of protest. Undoubtedly there are other people who feel as I do, but they first have to find one another, and here even that is not easy. The intelligentsia is afraid to write protest letters now or to sign them, after all the trials of writers and others we have had.

Most people here read the excerpts from the trials that are published in our press and they believe what they read. And when someone raises questions about what is really going on in these trials, they say, "Haven't you looked at the paper? It's written up there; it's all explained." That's the way most people here think. Even my close friends, who are intelligent, good fellows—they do not believe much of what is said at the political meetings we have to attend—always urge me, "Don't make an issue of it, just do as everyone else does." I was down on the beach in the south when we heard the

Tass announcement about our troops going into Czecho-slovakia [in 1968]. People gathered around a radio and listened, and their reaction was, "Well, the situation there must be very serious or we wouldn't have sent soldiers. Evidently it was necessary—the statement said so." And they went right back to playing dominos and sunning themselves. When I tried to argue with a few people that maybe it wasn't as straightforward as all that, they got so worked up and up-set with me that I finally had to break it off by dashing into the water.

CASES FROM THE

"CHRONICLE"

This document illustrates why it is so difficult for people with dissenting outlooks and reforming ideas "to find one another," as the young man in the preceding conversation put it, let alone for them to engage in concerted public protest. It is a description of arrests and interrogations of young people in Moscow in the last two months of 1969, one of many such accounts of political repressions, which are reported in the December 31, 1969, issue of Khronika tekushchikh sobytii *(Chronicle of Current Events), an underground bimonthly that has been appearing in Moscow since April, 1968.*

On November 20, 1969, the KGB [the security police, formally called the Committe on State Security] arrested Vyacheslav Vakhmin, a fourth-year student in the physics and chemistry department of the Moscow Institute of Physics Technology. Vakhmin is twenty-two years old and was a pupil at the Kolmogorov Boarding School (No. 18). He entered the institute in 1966. Ten days after his arrest, a search was made in the hostel where he was living; Vakhmin himself was not present at the time, and his friends at the hostel were told that he had gone away on a trip. (Now three weeks after his arrest, the authorities want to expel Vakhmin from the institute for failing to attend classes.)

The next day, December 1, searches were made simultaneously in six Moscow flats and two girl students were arrested: Irina Kaplun (third-year student at Moscow University, Philology Faculty, department of structural and applied linguistics), and Olga Ioffe (second-year student taking evening courses at Moscow University's Faculty of Economics). During the search, several items of *samizdat* were removed from Ioffe, and also her own poetry and paper; verses by her father, Yu. M. Ioffe; and a typewriter. The search was made in Ioffe's presence, and after it she was taken for questioning under an escort of ten men. At nine o'clock that evening a warrant for her arrest was signed.

On the same day, Irina Kaplun was taken for questioning. Earlier in the day when she was still in the university building she had been taken ill with heart trouble and had gone home. But she never reached her house. Evidently she was picked up on the way there and sent to the KGB without being taken home for a search first. The search was made while she was being interrogated. Removed from her were *samizdat* items, verses and stories by herself, a home-made anthology of poems by Yevtushenko, and a typewriter.

Both girls are nineteen years old. Olga Ioffe studied at Physics and Mathematics school No. 444, and Irina Kaplun at Special Language School No. 16. In 1966, both girls, with nine other pupils of the No. 16 school, all under sixteen years of age, pasted up leaflets, the content of which was as follows: There must be no repetition of the Stalin period; everything depends on us. About three hundred of these leaflets were pasted up and put into letterboxes of private dwellings in various districts of Moscow. Most of them were handed over to the KGB by the recipients. The main question put later to the children was: Tell us the names of the adults who organized this. The investigation was conducted by Major

Yeliseyev. School lessons alternated with interrogation sessions, which lasted from four to six hours. At the interrogations, the girls were told: "If you think some things in our country are not quite as they should be, then you ought to come and see us at the KGB and talk it over with us."

The case was not taken to court. After completion of the investigation, the school authorities took up the matter with the children. There were interviews and heart-to-heart talks with the district committee of the Komsomol. And it was always the same question: "Surely you can tell me, who were the adults involved?" All told, two children were expelled from the Komsomol, one from the school, and all of them were given reprimands with entries in their personal files. Two teachers were deprived of their right to teach, the school head was relieved of his post, and the class teachers were given reprimands and relieved of their duties as directors of their classes.

It is assumed that the arrest at this stage of I. Kaplun and O. Ioffe is connected with a protest they were preparing against the celebrations for the ninetieth birthday of Stalin.

On the same day, December 1, a fourth-year student at the Moscow State Institute of Historical Archives, Tatyana Khromova, was subjected to a search and interrogation. During the search, personal letters and a file containing poems by O. Mandelshtam were removed. They wanted to carry off her icons and were greatly interested in where she had obtained them, but after she had begged them at length, they agreed to leave them. They were interested to know if Khromova believed in God and why there were so many religious poems in her flat.

On December 5, Valeria Novotvorskaya was arrested in the Palace of Congresses, where she was scattering and handing out leaflets before the start of a performance of the opera *October*. Novotvorskaya made no attempt to escape and continued to hand out leaflets until she was approached by KGB men. The leaflets were written in the form of verses, and the theme was: our tanks in Czechoslovakia. There was probably also something in them about the constitution. After Novotvorskaya's arrest, several copies of three manuscript booklets of her own poetry were removed from her flat.

Valeria Novotvorskaya is nineteen. She finished school in 1968 with a medal and gained a place with honors in the French department of Foreign Languages Institute. At the time of her arrest she was in her second year there.

(Translated by Peter Reddaway)

BUKOVSKY'S STATEMENT

On January 22, 1967, three writers in their early and middle twenties—Vladimir Bukovsky, Vadim Delone, and Yevgeny Kushev—held a small demonstration in Moscow's Pushkin Square to call for a revision in the Criminal Code and to protest the arrest a few days earlier of another group of young Russians who had edited an underground magazine called Phoenix '66. Bukovsky, Delone, and Kushev were also arrested. Both groups were tried and their members received penalties ranging from a one-year suspended sentence to seven years' hard labor. Here are excerpts from the final statement Bukovsky made at his trial in September, 1967. It is worth reading attentively for the light it throws on the outlook and tactics of the young generation of serious protesters. Bukovsky describes the circumstances of his arrest on Pushkin Square and then goes on forcefully to document the point that he and his colleagues are being tried for defending freedoms that are guaranteed them by the Soviet constitution.

BUKOVSKY: Let me examine the essence of the case. Persons in civilian clothes, without armbands, called themselves *druzhinniki*, but only by their actions could one know that they were *druzhinniki*. *Druzhinniki* play a positive, serious role in the battle against crime—against thieves, hooligans, and so forth—at which time they always wear armbands. A basic rule of the *druzhinniki* requires that armbands be worn. But they didn't even show us their documents. When the *druzhinnik* Kleimenov, who appeared here as a witness, ran up to me, he cried: "What filth are you displaying? Now you'll get it in the eye."

Without a doubt, all this had been planned earlier; the people at the square knew about our demonstration beforehand. Indeed, militiaman Gruzinov did not appear to notice any violation of public order in the square and did not approach the demonstrators until some person in civilian clothes gave the order to seize one of us. Perhaps this person was a *druzhinnik*? No. How could an experienced militiaman not recognize a *druzhinnik* if he was wearing an armband? So who could this man have been? Just why did Gruzinov carry out the request of one private citizen to seize another who had not disturbed the peace. Obviously, he had been previously instructed, and evidently his instructions were sufficiently specific.

Colonel Abramov of the KGB arrived at the square, certainly not as a private citizen. It is not likely that he was out for a stroll, which is not one of his habits. Wrongfully, the court did not call him as a witness, for he could have told things about the case no less important than the statements of the other witnesses.

Note that so far I have not used the word, but it seems that this was a *provocation*. In fact, what else could one call it?

In our country, the organs of state security play a police role. What democracy can there be to speak of when we are being watched? Let them catch spies! Why are we being questioned about our acquaintances, about what we were doing two or three years ago, and so forth? I recognize the important role of the KGB in the fight for state security.

But what is their business in this case? There were no external enemies involved here. Perhaps they had internal ones in mind. There were no grounds for the interference of the state security organs, but let's take a look at how our case was handled. Why did they have to drag it [the investigation] out for a period of seven months? And by the way, why did they put us at once in investigatory isolation cells of the KGB? I won't distract the court's attention by describing the conditions in the isolation cell block—but there certainly is a difference. In the isolation cell block there are two or three of us in a cell, whereas in ordinary prison cells there are seven to eight persons. If you have to stay there several months, it has its effects on a person's mental state.

JUDGE: Defendant Bukovsky, this is of no interest to us; keep closer to the indictment. What relevance does everything you are saying have, essentially, to the resolution of your case?

BUKOVSKY: I have already said that you have no right to interrupt me.

There have been breaches of the law in the conduct of the investigation, and it is my duty to speak out about them, so now I am speaking out.

We demonstrated in defense of legality. It is incomprehensible why the office whose responsibility it is to safeguard the rights of citizens sanctions such actions by the *druzhinniki* and the KGB.

Now I have to explain our slogans. The demonstration was conducted with a slogan demanding the freeing of Galanskov, Dobrovolsky, Lashkova, and Radziyevsky. But they have not even been convicted yet. What if it turns out that they are not guilty? In fact, Radziyevsky has already been released from custody. Then where is the criminality of demonstration?

Now as to our second slogan? We did not come out against laws. We demanded the abrogation of the decree of September 16 and the revision of Article 70 of the Criminal Code. Was this really an illegal action on our part? We protested against an unconstitutional decree. Was this really an anti-Soviet demand? We are not alone in finding the decree unconstitutional. A group of representatives of the intelligentsia, among them Academician Leontovich, the writer Kaverin, and others, have presented a similar demand to the Presidium of the Supreme Soviet of the U.S.S.R.

Isn't the Constitution the basic law of our country? I shall read the full text of Article 125:

In conformity with the interests of the working people, and in order to strengthen the socialist system, the citizens of the U.S.S.R. are guaranteed by law:

  a) freedom of speech;
  b) freedom of the press;
  c) freedom of assembly, including the holding of mass meetings;
  d) freedom of street processions and demonstrations.

These civil rights are ensured by placing at the disposal of the working people and their organizations printing presses, stocks of paper, public buildings, the streets—

Yes, the streets, citizen prosecutor!
"—communications facilities and other material requisites for the exercise of these rights."

Now, about Article 70. We demanded its revision because it is subject to too broad an interpretation. Here is the text:

Agitation or propaganda carried on for the purpose of subverting or weakening Soviet authority or of committing certain especially dangerous crimes against the state, or circulating for the same purpose slanderous fabrications that defame the Soviet state and social system, or circulating, preparing, or keeping, for the same purpose, literature of such content, shall be punished by deprivation of freedom for a term of six months to seven years, with or without additional exile for a term of two to five years, or by exile for a term of two to five years.

Article 70 contains such heterogeneous things as agitation and propaganda aiming at the commission of particularly dangerous state crimes and, on the other hand, slanderous statements against the social system. The range of penalties is also too wide—from half a year to seven years. In the annotations and interpretations of the Code, this article is divided into fourteen points. It would seem that revision of the article ought to follow this guideline, making the penalties more specific, too.

This would lessen its arbitrary nature.

JUDGE: Defendant Bukovsky, we are lawyers here, and all those present in the courtroom have also been through grammar school. We realize that you have just now been exposed to problems of the law and have become interested in them. We applaud this interest, but it is unnecessary to discuss them at such length here. Understand: We must decide the question of your guilt or innocence, decide your fate. Possibly you will enter Moscow University as a student of law. There at the seminars you shall discuss these questions on a higher level.

BUKOVSKY: No, I won't enter. And I object to the prosecutor's accusing us of legal illiteracy and a lack of seriousness. No, I do know the laws, and I speak of them seriously. If, however, what I am speaking about is so well known, it is even more incomprehensible why the prosecutor sees criticism of the law as a crime.

The preamble of Article 125 of the Constitution says: "In conformity with the interests of the working people, and in order to strengthen the socialist system, the citizens of the U.S.S.R. are guaranteed by law—"

It is completely clear that neither legally nor grammatically is it possible to interpret this preamble as meaning that the freedoms listed in this article, including the freedom of meetings and demonstrations, are permitted only on condition that they be exercised with the aims mentioned in this preamble.

Freedom of speech and of the press is, first of all, freedom to criticize. Nobody has ever forbidden praise of the government. If there are in the constitution articles about freedom of speech and of the press, then have the patience to listen to criticism. In what kinds of countries is it forbidden to criticize the government and to protest against its actions? Perhaps in capitalist countries? No, we know that in bourgeois countries Communist Parties exist whose purpose it is to undermine the capitalist system. In the U.S.A., the Communist Party was suppressed. However, the Supreme Court declared that the suppression was unconstitutional and restored the Communist Party to its full rights.

JUDGE: Bukovsky, this does not have any relevance to the accusations in your case.

A few brief exchanges between Bukovsky and the judge are omitted here.

BUKOVSKY: You are judges. You are supposed to embody these qualities. If you actually embody honesty and integrity, you will render the only possible verdict in this case—a verdict of "not guilty." I realize that this is very difficult.

PROSECUTOR (interrupting): I direct the attention of the court to the fact that the accused is abusing his right to make a final statement. He criticizes the law, discredits the activities of the organs of the KGB, and is beginning to insult you— a new criminal act is being perpetrated here. As a representative of the prosecution, I must stop this, and I call upon you to require the defendant to talk only about the substance of the charges against him. Otherwise, one might listen endlessly here to speeches containing all kinds of criticism of the laws and of the government.

JUDGE: Defendant Bukovsky, you have heard the prosecutor's remarks. I will permit you to speak only on the substance of the indictment.

BUKOVSKY (to the prosecutor): You accuse us of trying, by our slogans, to discredit the KGB, but the KGB has so discredited itself that we have nothing to add. (To the court:) I shall speak about the charges. But what the prosecutor would like to hear from me he will not hear. There is no criminal act in our case. I absolutely do not repent having organized this demonstration. I find that it accomplished what it had to accomplish, and when I am free again, I shall again organize demonstrations—of course, in complete accordance with the laws, as before. I have finished my statement.

In Quest of Justice: Protest and Dissent in the Soviet Union Today, edited by Abraham Brumberg, New York: Praeger Publishers, 1970

THE KGB TALKS

WITH LITVINOV

It was Pavel Litvinov, the grandson of former Soviet Foreign Minister Maxim Litvinov, who saw to it that the transcript of Bukovsky's final statement reached Western sources. When the KGB learned of Litvinov's plan to publicize the Bukovsky trial, he was summoned for interrogation.

I regard it as my duty to bring the following to the knowledge of the public:

On September 26, 1967, I was summoned by the KGB to appear before Gostev, a KGB official, at 2 Derzhinsky Square, Room 537. Another official of the KGB, who did not give his name, was present during our conversation.

After this talk was over, I wrote it down immediately and as fully as I could remember because I am certain that it clearly revealed tendencies which should be made public, and which cannot but alarm our progressive society and the world in general. The text of the conversation follows. I vouch for the accuracy of the substance of what was said between the KGB official and myself.

GOSTEV: Pavel Mikhailovich, we have knowledge that you and a group of other persons intend to reproduce and distribute the minutes of the recent criminal trial of Bukovsky and others. We warn you that if you do, you will be held criminally responsible.

I: Irrespective of my intentions, I cannot understand what the criminal responsibility for such action might be.

GOSTEV: The court will decide that. We only wish to warn you that if such a record should be disseminated in Moscow or other cities, or should appear abroad, you will be made responsible for it.

I: I know the laws well, and I cannot imagine what particular law would be violated by the compilation of such a document.

GOSTEV: There is such a law—Article 190-1. Take the Criminal Code and read it.

I: I know the article very well and can recite it from memory. It deals with slanderous fabrications which would discredit the Soviet social system and regime. What kind of slander could there be in recording the hearing of a case before a Soviet court?

GOSTEV: Well, your notes will be a biased distortion of the facts and a slander of the court's actions, as would be proved by the agency competent to handle such cases.

I: How can you possibly know this? And in general, instead of conducting this senseless talk and starting a new case, you yourself should publish the record of this criminal trial and in this way kill the rumors circulating in Moscow. Yesterday I met an acquaintance and she told me such a lot of nonsense about the trial that it was simply disgusting to listen to it.

GOSTEV: And why do we need to publish it? It is an ordinary criminal case of disturbance of the peace.

I: If so, it is all the more important to give information— to let all the people see it's really an ordinary case.

GOSTEV: *Vechernyaya Moskva* [the newspaper *Evening Moscow*] of September 4, 1967, gives all the information about the case. All that has to be known about the trial is reported there.

I: In the first place, too little information is given; a reader who had heard nothing previously about the case would simply not understand what it was all about. In the second place, [the newspaper report] is false and slanderous. Rather, the editor of *Vechernyaya Moskva*, or the person who provided such information, should be charged with slander.

GOSTEV: Pavel Mikhailovich, this information is entirely correct. Remember that.

I: It says that Bukovsky pleaded guilty. Yet I, who was interested in this case, know perfectly well that he did not plead guilty.

GOSTEV: What does it matter whether he pleaded guilty or not? The court found him guilty; so he *is* guilty.

*The interrogation continued for a while and then
ended with the following exchange.*

GOSTEV: Pavel Mikhailovich, we have no intention of arguing with you. We simply warn you. Just imagine if people should learn that the grandson of the great diplomat Litvinov is busy with such doings—it would be a blot on his memory.

I: Well, I do not think he would blame me. Can I go?

GOSTEV: Please. The best thing for you to do now would be to go home and destroy everything you have collected.

In Quest of Justice

A LETTER FROM
TWENTY-FOUR STUDENTS

Early in January, 1968, the group of people who had edited Phoenix '66 *went on trial. As sentence was being passed on them, Pavel Litvinov and Larisa Daniel (the wife of Yuli Daniel, a writer who was then serving a five-year sentence in a labor camp) issued an open letter to world public opinion denouncing the trial as a "wild mockery" of the accused. The next day, twenty-four Moscow high school students who agreed with this assessment of the trial sent a letter to Litvinov expressing their feelings about the treatment of Russia's writers.*

Dear Pavel Mikhailovich:

Thank you and Larisa Daniel for your brave and honest letter. We are revolted to the depths of our souls by the trial, and we understand what general silence and apathy can lead to. We began to see things clearly two years ago. When Sinyavsky and Daniel were convicted, we realized the crying injustice of our organs of power and the cruelty of individuals who mockingly trample upon the literary and human rights of people

Our fathers and grandfathers were shot or died in camps; they knew all the horrors of Stalinist reaction. We can imagine how terrible it is to live surrounded by silence and fear. Therefore the thinking generation of the 1960's calls upon all people of integrity to support these two courageous individuals by signing their names to our letter. He who keeps silent commits a crime against his conscience and against Russia. And Russia pays dearly for this with the blood of her most intelligent and talented people, from Osip Mandelshtam to Aleksandr Ginzburg. We are for the publication of Brodsky's verses, Romisov's and Zamiatin's stories, the poetry of the late Mandelshtam, and the prose of Pasternak. We are for the release of Sinyavsky and Daniel; we favor a re-examination of the case of the four writers by an international tribunal in accordance with international law; we favor a severe admonition to the courts to restore the norms of socialist legality. We despise Dobrovolsky's vile treachery; he is nothing other than a Smerdiakov. We who are just emerging into life are already fed up with hypocrisy and deceit—we want truth and justice.

Only united can we succeed in accomplishing something; otherwise worse will follow: terror, reaction, innocent sacrifice. For we are responsible for all that happens in the world— after all, we are taught this by the best works of our literature. We cannot resign ourselves to the narrow-minded interpretations of Tolstoy, Chekhov, Kuprin, Blok, or to the exclusion of Dostoyevsky, Bunin, Tsvetaeva, Pasternak and others from the school curriculum. Our schools have produced reliable *okhranniki* [watchmen]—stupid crammers who study the history of the Party and the fundamentals of historical materialism. We cannot keep silent when demagogy, journalistic lies, and deceit are all around. We are only sorry for our parents. We request that this letter be circulated so that it may reach those who are our own age and think as we do, and so that the fate of these writers will be justly decided.

We hope that despite everything we are not alone, and that we will hear the voices of upright people.

[*signed by twenty-four students*]

Moscow: January 13, 1968

In Quest of Justice

BACKLASH

Litvinov also received some critical and even hostile responses from Russians with no sympathy for the protest movement. Here are excerpts from two of them. Letters such as these are often initiated by the authorities as part of a deliberate backlash against dissent. While there is no way of knowing whether or not that is the case in these two instances, it can be said that there are many people in Russia who feel as do this engineer and this "ordinary Soviet woman," as she describes herself in the letter. These people are unfamiliar with the concepts of freedom and justice that animate the dissenters and have a deep-rooted Russian feeling that it is wrong to expose Soviet internal problems to world, particularly Western, attention. Both selections appeared in Letters and Telegrams to Pavel Litvinov, *first published by D. Reidel Publishing Company, Dordrecht, the Netherlands, 1969.*

Narva
January 20, 1968

Citizen Litvinov.

I heard the series of broadcasts on the radio of our "friends" about the trial of the "writers" and your conduct at the trial. I must express to you my indignation at you. You have disgraced the name of your father, or your grandfather

(I don't know exactly how you are related to Foreign Affairs Commissar M. Litvinov). He was a man whom I have read a lot about and about whom I collect information as about our other commissars. Your appeal to foreigners is base and vile. Our only mistake was not to expel Sinyavsky and D. [Daniel] from the country, instead of imprisoning them.

If you're not satisfied with our policy, go to the devil. What is needed is work, with hand and brain, and not a lot of nonsensical talk; we need more strictness, like we used to have, then there will be more order, better production. Today too many people discuss and say what should and should not be done, and work goes forward too slowly.

[. . .]—construction engineer and engineering economist, 31

P.S. Take into account that I live among the people, ordinary folk, these who are called the "plodders," and I know better than you what people need.

January 5, 1968

To Litvinov's grandson.

This letter is written to you by an ordinary Soviet woman, not a Party member, who has experienced much, known hunger and cold, during both the Civil War and the Patriotic War, who has known the taste of bread earned by her own toil, and known what it is to draw ten rubles from the mutual-help fund in order to last out till payday. But all these are mere trifles beside the irremediable misfortune I have suffered with my only child—my son has been confined to his bed for many years now and will never be able to walk.

Suppose somebody said to me: "Tomorrow your son will get up and walk, go skiing, be able to go to the woods, to the theater, wherever he likes, and know all the joys of life; for this to happen, only a trifle is needed, namely that you write a libel on the Soviet regime and send it to foreign journal-

ists." I should not consider such a suggestion for even one
second, I should reply simply, without any dramatics—never!

But you, to whom the Soviet regime has given everything,
for whom from infancy all roads have been open, you who
have always been able to go wherever you wanted, who could
choose whatever university you liked, who have always enjoyed material security, who were given a flat by the Moscow
municipality without having to wait your turn, and a flat
within the Garden Ring at that, you who have made a habit
of capitalizing on your forefathers' services, and all for
nothing, taking all the good things of life as your due, you
unhesitatingly write a libel on the Soviet regime and send
it to filthy journalists to be used in a filthy broadcast by the
"Voice of America," and even declare that your grandfather would have approved of you. How dare you speak for
your grandfather! All his life he fought for peace and
security for the Soviet people, but you are pouring oil on the
fires of war that are already blazing.—

In the name of all mothers of disabled children,

[*signed*]

THE DUTY OF

A COMMUNIST

*One of the most outspoken comments on the
Moscow trials of 1967 and 1968 came from a man
who up to that time had been thoroughly "establishment" in his position—Ivan Yakhimovich,
who was then the chairman of a collective farm
and a member of the Communist Party. In a
letter in February, 1968, to one of the top Soviet
leaders, which he considered it "the duty of a
Communist" to write, he expressed this view.*

I believe that the persecution of young dissenters in
a country where more than 50 per cent of the population
are younger than thirty years of age is an extremely dangerous line—adventurism. It is not the toadies, not a public of
yes men (O Lord, how they have multiplied!), not the
mama's boys who will determine our future, but rather those
very rebels, the most energetic, brave, and high-principled
members of our young generation.

It is stupid to see in them the enemies of Soviet power,
and more than stupid to let them rot in prisons and to mock
them. For the party, such a line is equivalent to self-strangu-
lation. Too bad for us if we are not capable of reaching an
understanding with these young people. They will create,
inevitably they will create, a new party. Ideas cannot be
murdered with bullets, prisons, or exile. He who does not
understand this is no politician, no Marxist.

In Quest of Justice

High school students

PART NINE

Jobs and Ambitions

Soviet young people have a tremendous drive to get an education and move upward. This is the whole thrust of the society they live in, and sixteen-year-old Natasha reflects it well when she says, in Part Two, "I suppose the thing we most want is knowledge, because now we are grown up and we understand that nothing can be done without knowledge." Knowledge gives the young people access to the prestige jobs to which they aspire—as doctors and scientists and engineers—and it opens up to them a different way of life, which they perceive to be more comfortable, glamorous, and civilized. This great upward thrust of education is one of the striking developments of the last fifty years, and it is to be felt at all levels of the society. A good industrial worker, for example, is often not content to remain a worker—he takes night courses so he can become an engineer. And his son will probably reach even higher, to become a scientist. By now, close to one-half of Soviet youngsters receive a complete high school education, and the goal of the 1970's is to make it universal. It is not surprising that an effort to raise a whole population so drastically should have its problems at the *level of the individual, and that is what this chapter is mostly about. But first of all, to give you a sense of how people have had career opportunities opened up to them, and often thrust upon them, by the great turmoil of Russia's revolution and industrialization, here are glimpses into several people's working lives over the years.*

RUSSIAN HORATIO ALGERS

"My name is Dmitri Pestoon," he began. "I'm seventy-eight years old and was born in Petrograd. I began to work in a factory when I was still a youngster. I took part in the revolutionary struggle.

"When the Civil War ended I was called to the regional committee of the Party, which had just been formed—Ivan Shchipovskikh was the secretary at the time. There they said to me: 'Comrade Pestoon, we've got to build the country all over again. We must build our industry, must buy machines, and we need gold for that. You'll be director of the Lena gold fields.'

"I didn't know a single thing about gold mining. But nobody else did either. Most of the specialists had either fled or sat waiting at home for the Soviet Government to fall apart. Bandits, ruin, and hunger—that's all you saw around you. I made plenty of mistakes at first, using my tongue instead of my head. But then I learned what to do, and things took a turn for the better. That was when I decided to become a mining engineer."

"But we had other plans," Shchipovskikh interrupted. "We wanted him to become a schoolteacher. That was in the twenties, when we needed workers desperately. The country was simply choking, if I can put it that way. It needed everything: gold, machines, tractors, bread, textbooks. And so we Communists began to learn one specialty after another. Not because we wanted to, but because we had to. Dmitri Pestoon was an engineer, a builder and a teacher."

Soviet Life, February, 1966

There is one anniversary Vladimir Promyslov never thinks to celebrate, the turning point in his life, that day in the summer of 1924 when he arrived in Moscow. A peasant boy of sixteen who knew only the wooden plow and the pitchfork, he came to learn a fitter's trade in the city of which he is now the mayor.

But the first job, which actually decided his future, was on the construction of a settlement near Moscow's Abelmanovsksy Gate.

At the early age of twenty he joined the Party, and at the late age of thirty-three graduated from the Civil Engineering Institute where he now teaches. This was very characteristic of Soviet intellectuals of the first generation. They were self-made, mostly self-taught men. Their fathers and grandfathers were illiterate.

USSR, November, 1964

My life as a full-fledged doctor did not begin well. I was late for the graduation party. An argument with Mother about whether the dress I had made needed a bow or not ended with the usual reproach: "We spend our lives bringing up our children, only to find that when they grow up they don't need us any more."

When I finally got there, the girls told me my graduation diploma had been handed to my husband and added slyly, "You'll be under a male thumb for the rest of your life." My diploma and my husband's were on the top of the list, since our name begins with an "A" and we both were awarded diplomas with honors.

The graduation party was the dividing line between the student days behind us and the medical career ahead of us.

We already had our assignments and were packing to go to Siberia, to the town of Ust-Kut, a port on the Lena.

In our final year at the Astrakhan Medical College, which has a good reputation, requests for graduates kept pouring in from all over the country to the college committee responsible for assigning people. There were requests for doctors right there in Astrakhan itself, but we were bent on going to Siberia, for two reasons. My own was a very practical one—I wanted a place where earnings were high. I had grown up in a family of three sisters and a brother. My father was killed in the war [World War II], and my mother had had a hard time bringing us up. I was tired of wearing my elder sisters' castoffs and wanted very much to give mother a chance to quit work and take it easy. Valentin, my husband, was drawn to Siberia because he hoped he would be on his own and do big things.

Soviet Life, February, 1966

"It's not a bad prospect at all," said Nikolai Sureyev from the Building Institute. "I asked to be sent to some out-of-the-way place. What are my chances in Moscow? That in five years' time I'll head a team of engineers and make about 180 rubles a month. I can't see any farther than that. But out in the wilds, where they're building a factory, I could get to be chief engineer in two years. Then, if I wanted to come back to Moscow, I could come back a king instead of just a pawn."

Sureyev is one of those young people who is out to make a career for himself. He wants to get to the top, where the pay is good and there is more opportunity to apply his brains and knowledge, as fast as he can.

Soviet Life, May, 1966

Tatyana is a graceful twenty-two-year-old. . . .

She is a copyist in a plant design bureau and a third-year student in the Machine-tool Institute's evening division. She has classes four times a week, from 4:30 to 7:40, and therefore only three free evenings—Thursday, Saturday, and Sunday.

"Don't you find it hard?"

"Well, yes. But I manage. It helps when conditions for studying are so good. The branch of the institute I attend is next to the plant; I can see it from my office window. I get additional paid leave to prepare for exams: Twenty days for the first three years, and forty for the last three. My summer vacations are six weeks long.

"And then for me, personally, it's so much easier to study because Anatoli, my boy friend, is taking the same courses."

"What does he do?"

"He's a machine-tool designer. He finished technical school and is very good at his job, but he wants to get an engineering degree." Tatyana will be getting hers in four years.

USSR, July, 1964

A WOMAN CONSTRUCTION

WORKER

Here is a girl who has an unglamorous job. After leaving school, she went to work at a construction site in the Ural Mountains, at the western edge of Siberia. In Russia it is not unusual for young women to work on building projects, doing unskilled or low-skill labor that is often physically demanding and offers them little opportunity for advancement. There is a problem here that has been recognized and discussed in the Soviet press, but for the time being the society needs the labor of these women—there are simply not enough willing men to handle all the construction jobs. You get some feeling for what it is like to arrive out there, fresh from school, in these excerpts from the diary of eighteen-year-old Ludmilla Pirozhkova, published in Komsomolskaya pravda *(Young Communist League Truth) on October 29, 1969.*

I'm going to work on a construction site. That's how things have worked out. I was short one point for getting into the university. I'm afraid not of the work but of the cold. It's a weakness, one that is fully explainable. I lived five years in Frunze [in Kirgizia, Central Asia], never experiencing winter—and suddenly, here I am in the Urals, winter up to my ears.

Why have I come here to the construction site? I had to settle somewhere, get registered, and earn a living. I went into the *obkom* [the province committee of the Komsomol] office just by chance, to see what they had to offer. And after a conversation with the *obkom* fellows, I stayed on. They didn't idealize things and didn't propagandize. Right away, it somehow became not "their" construction site, but "ours."

I realized that to run away immediately would just not be possible. Maybe they'll fire me. Or maybe they won't reproach me very much either. Only now do I understand that those who fled from the Virgin Lands were not complete scoundrels, but simply people. Perhaps they were even good people, capable of heroic deeds in other circumstances. Maybe their health required some rest. Maybe their dreams pulled them to a factory shop or to a library, to books. Maybe, maybe. There are many variations. But nonetheless, they are deserters. No, I'm not afraid of it's being hard. If only I don't break down and don't have to take to my bed— that's the main thing. Don't let me down, comrade health!

Tomorrow is the first of September [when Soviet schools open]. A day that is always exciting. Now it doesn't affect me one bit. All that seems far away, far away. But still and all, tomorrow is a very big day for me—I'm starting a job! Hello there, construction site! Happiness. It doesn't call out from the corner, "Yoo-hoo, here I am!" It doesn't jump out from the corner and throw itself on your neck. That's why it isn't easy for people to find it. And sometimes it's downright difficult. And another thing: It's impossible to find a "ready-made," "synthetic," "universal" happiness. For each person it is different.

The mortar is frozen stiff. It crumbles but doesn't break

off. The tool in the hand is as unwieldy as a rifle. A fine dust flies into your eyes. If only they don't notice that I'm no good at this.

Hit it! Hit! One chip flies and then another. That's how it goes. You have to swing the hack easily. Hold it with your hands firmly, so that when it falls, it doesn't swerve. Otherwise you waste your energy.

So it's a little physics and some experience. Swing, hit. Hit, a chip. Another blow, another chip.

This next part is unscientific: With every chip that's knocked off, my strength grows. I *can* do this!

Annushka, Annushka. She's enough to drive you crazy— a difficult, stubborn person. You just can't tell whether there's more bad or good in her. I always want things to be definite, good or bad. She often swears. And then suddenly, a kind of dogged diligence about her work. We're lugging planks. I'm tired—if only I could sit down. But doggedly, she is dragging whole logs, dogged and silent. And she doesn't rest.

Today is the end of the shift. There are three of us. And a heap of clay for making cement. "Shall we carry it over?" That's Annushka.

"Are you kidding? You mean we should stay on after five o'clock?" That's red-haired Liudka.

Annushka doesn't say anything. But five minutes later there comes once again, "Shall we finish the job?"

"All right, let's. I'll go along with you." Even Liudka agrees. We work in a hurry. The clay flies out from under our feet. The insecurely nailed boards shake.

We've finished.

There is a hardly noticeable but contented smile on Annushka's lips. "That's how you have to work. Until I got here, they were sitting around doing nothing."

WHO WILL DO

THE UNPOPULAR JOBS?

To be a member of the intelligentsia—the people who have a higher education or at least an extended post-secondary one—is the aspiration of the great majority of high school students. So high do many of them aspire that the Soviet press of late has been trying to dampen down their career expectations a bit, pointing out that the society needs people to do the unpopular jobs as well as the glamorous ones. This excerpt, representing the official view, is from a booklet entitled Young People: About Themselves and Their Contemporaries, *published in 1969. It is the result of research by a group of Leningrad sociologists.*

Research has shown that the most popular professions among Soviet young people are those of cosmonaut, theoretical physicist, test pilot, and physician.

The majority of high school graduates want to become doctors, chemists, physicists, and engineers. In theory, this is as it should be. But one is perfectly justified in asking, who is going to grow the grain and bake the bread and stitch the shoes and cook the dinner? What do we do with the principle, "I don't like the work, but it has to be done."

A contradiction has arisen: On the one hand there is the

unpopularity of the service occupations among the young, and on the other there is the acute necessity, already now, to send into retail trade and into restaurant and catering work four times as many young people as we send into agriculture and twice as many as go into industry. During this five-year plan, the volume of everyday services should increase two and a half times, while industrial production is to grow by forty percent. There is food for thought here.

Sociological research shows that the overwhelming majority of boys and girls dream of doing work that is creative.

In school and at home children are told, "If you do well at your studies, all roads will be open to you. You can choose any profession!" The youngsters want not "any" profession, but an "interesting" one. But so far, not today, not tomorrow and not the day after tomorrow will we be in a position to guarantee to everyone work that is creative. There is now and there still will be for a long time to come a number of professions that are not creative and attractive but are still necessary to the society.

In some families and schools, unfortunately, they talk to the children often and at length about "superintelligent" machines that do everything for people, about how in the future they will have only to push a button to get a finished product. This develops an incorrect and distorted notion about work.

Need one say what enormous moral harm such upbringing will do to the young people when in the future they meet reality and become convinced that in life, as on a train, there are more hard seats than soft ones. Disillusionment sets in, and a lack of faith, and a skeptical attitude toward present-day life.

WHO GOES TO THE UNIVERSITY?:

SOME STATISTICS

FROM GORKY

It is the case in the Soviet Union, as in other parts of the world, that where you live—whether in city or village—and what social group of the population you belong to have a good deal to do with your chances of finishing high school and reaching the university. This information on what happens to children in the city of Gorky is drawn from an article by Vladimir Kantorovich in Novy mir *(New World), No. 12, 1967.*

In the city of Gorky, for example, 80 per cent of the children in the younger grades come from workers' families and 20 per cent are the children of people in the professions and in office work, percentages corresponding to the actual composition of the city's population. In the upper grades there is an increasing drop-out of workers' children from school. In the highest grade (by comparison with the lowest ones), the proportion of children of professional people and office workers is considerably above this groups's proportion in the over-all city population. Moreover, the more education the father and mother have had and the greater the family's prosperity, the better the pupil does in school.

Of those graduating from high school, the children of the

urban intelligentsia are primarily the ones who get into the university and the institute. A study of high school graduates in each social group of the population showed that 82 per cent of the children of the urban intelligentsia went on with their studies [presumably all kinds of study—day, evening, and correspondence], 61 per cent of the children of industrial workers went on, 46 per cent of the children of people who work in consumer services, and only 10 per cent of the children of agricultural workers (because of the low level of teaching in village schools).

Waiting to take entrance examinations for the Physics Faculty at Moscow University   (*Soviet Life*)

WHAT ARE THE SCHOOLS
PREPARING PEOPLE FOR?

As growing numbers of people receive a full high school education, the chances of getting into the university and institute will become harder, and more disappointed youths will have to take jobs in industry for which they are psychologically and culturally unprepared. That prospect is the general theme of the article from which these two excerpts are drawn. Written by a team of manpower experts at Moscow University, it appeared in the Literaturnaya gazeta (Literary Gazette) *on July 3, 1968.*

Before 1953 the high schools graduated fewer people than the universities and institutes needed. So naturally the school curriculum was oriented toward the university. All high school graduates who wanted to go to college had the opportunity to do so. But in 1954 the number of high school graduates increased sharply, and in 1956–58 it was already twice as many as there were places for in the institutes and universities. It was then, in the mid-1950's, that really for the first time there appeared in industry young people with a complete high school education. And it was discovered that they were psychologically unprepared for ordinary work. People started to talk about the alienation of the secondary school from life, and then came a period of school reforms and experiments with vocational training [under Khrushchev].

In the first half of the 1960's, the population slump from the wartime years returned the educational system to its old course. Three and a half million high school graduates had gone to work in industry and then transferred over into the universities and institutes with the privileges that ensued from a two-year work stint. By this time, the school reforms had subsided and the schools settled down once again to preparing future university students.

Now, however, the competitive pressure of university entrance exams has revived, making it necessary to raise the requirements for those seeking entrance to the university. Between high school and the university there is developing a whole supplementary system of coaching and preparatory courses.

Once again, the universities and higher institutes cannot accept all the products of the high schools. What are the schools turning out these days? Candidates for the university? Only in part. What else? Future well-educated workers? If so, then why do the psychological mood and orientation of these graduates not correspond to this goal?

In 1966, of the young people who started work at the Moscow factory for the production of small cars, 10 per cent had completed high school, 56 per cent had completed the eighth grade, and 34 per cent were drop-outs after the fifth, sixth, and seventh grades.

We tried to analyze what kind of worker is most valuable to the factory. In the commissions for labor placement under the executive committees of the local Soviets, they consider the norm to be nothing less than a full high school education [through the tenth grade]. But in the factory, people look at it differently. There they evaluate someone by how well he takes root at his job and by his output. The main thing in the evaluation is not a lot of education but the sum

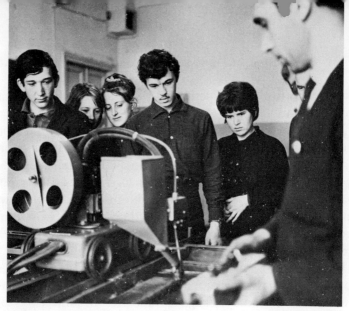

Vocational training   (*Novosti*)

of a person's qualities, so to speak—all the facts about him—
his sex, education, age, skills, working experience, military
service and so forth.

We circulated a questionnaire among the heads of the
different shops in the factory (assembling, painting, chassis,
instruments), among the foremen, and in the personnel
office:

"What level of education is sufficient for a person to do
the work in your section or in your shop?"

"If you could choose, who would you prefer to take on:
someone who has completed the tenth grade, the eighth
grade, or just the fifth or sixth grade?"

"Underline what you notice first when you take on a
newcomer to the job." (There followed a list of all the
various qualities, including "education.")

And so forth.

It turned out that education is far from the top of the list;
it came after age, military service, special skills, and other
considerations that are more significant to the factory people.

Only one-fourth of those questioned expressed a preference for people with a complete high school education; the others preferred workers who had only completed eighth grade or less. And it is interesting that in answer to the question, "How much education is enough?" (we stressed that we meant "enough," and not how much is desirable), only 7 per cent of those questioned gave the answer "a complete high school education"; 30 per cent said eight grades were enough and 68 per cent said seven were enough. The desired norm for a factory worker is an eighth-grade education. Why are they less happy in the factory with someone who has more schooling?

First of all, one has to keep in mind the category of people we questioned—foremen and shop managers, who are all practical people. What they expect above all from a newcomer on the job is a sense of responsibility and the desire to work.

Those who have finished high school come to this factory, as a rule, only after they have unsuccessfully tried to get into college.

For someone who has taken a college entrance exam and failed, having to work at a machine and on an assembly line is a misfortune in life. So it is understandable that the factory people prefer those young people who are not looking beyond the gates of the factory. The job of the section heads and shop managers is to fulfill the plan and not to discuss the all-round development of personality. Of course, they have a narrowly utilitarian approach in evaluating education. On the other hand, one must bear in mind that their judgments reflect two sides of the same problem: the fact that the factory is not yet everywhere ready to receive young people with a high level of education, and the fact that the schools graduate boys and girls who are psychologically unprepared to work in industry.

CHOOSING A PROFESSION

The magazine Yunost (Youth) *has been running a casual and occasional discussion on the subject of "choosing a profession," in the course of which the main uncertainty some of the readers have expressed is whether to push on with their studies when they are not yet sure what they want to become. Here are excerpts from three installments of the discussion (No. 1, 1968, No. 12, 1968, and No. 6, 1969), beginning with a letter from a girl explaining why she is dropping out of school for the time being.*

Dear Editors!

My name is Zhenya. I am a student in a tekhnikum [a specialized secondary school] in the chemistry department. I live in the dormitory.

In two days the director will sign an order expelling me from the school.

What happened was that when I entered my department a year and a half ago (I am already in the second year), I knew almost nothing about my specialty. The first year they didn't tell us anything about it. They said we would be working in a refinery, in chemical laboratories, and in chemical plants.

In school I despised chemistry. So why did I come here? I simply wanted to see if I could do it.

In the first year I did rather well in chemistry. But somehow I wasn't drawn to the subject—I felt indifferent toward it. During the second year this became even more noticeable. And now I am paying for my thoughtlessness.

When I said I wanted to leave the tekhnikum, my homeroom teacher replied that this was madness, that I must without fail graduate from the tekhnikum, that in a very short time I will be a specialist. Well, what kind of a specialist will I be if I am not at all interested in my specialty? How can I work well if I don't love my work?

When I said I was leaving the tekhnikum simply because I don't love my profession, many people were astonished. They go on studying even though they don't like the specialty either.

What will I do next? I'll get a job and go to night school, get my diploma, and then I'll enter an institute. But not a chemical institute.

Why have I written all this? I've told you about myself because those who feel as I do are many. Something should be done to change this situation. Maybe somebody else will give some thought to this.—With greetings, Zhenya K.

Following Zhenya's letter was a comment from a Yunost *correspondent, saying, in part:*

I personally think that one doesn't necessarily have to go to an institute right after graduation from high school—if, of course, a person has no definite, clearly expressed inclinations. To study for a year or two and then drop out of the institute is a hard thing to do, and it's terrible, but to drag out your discontentment is still worse, because this already spoils your life. Give yourself the opportunity of choosing. Not a profession, but an interest in life.

This advice from the Yunost *correspondent brought a cynical response from a man who signed his letter "M. Levinov, engineer, thirty-*

three years old (who graduated from an institute
that was not his first choice and is not even work-
ing in the field for which he was trained)." Here
are excerpts from his letter.

Let us look the truth in the eye. Ours is a time of statistics
and facts and of a scientific approach. Let's assume that 6
million pupils will graduate from the tenth grade in 1969
(all figures cited by the author are just approximate.—The
editors). The institutes will admit about 700,000–800,000
people. Consequently, only every sixth or seventh high
school graduate will enter an institute. Under these conditions it is ridiculous to say that you don't have to hurry to
get to the institute, that you should work for a while and
choose the profession you like, and so forth. No, you do
have to hurry, otherwise it will be too late: Your fresh
knowledge from school will be forgotten, your mind will
grow rusty as it gets unaccustomed to study, you'll be drawn
into a new life and have to get settled into it, and a year or
two (in effect doing whatever comes along, wherever it may
be) won't help you at all to find out what profession you
like. And isn't it time to stop this baby talk that each person
can find a profession that he likes, and that all professions
are interesting, and the main problem is to understand
what attracts you.

Let us not deceive the young people. Let's turn once again
to the facts, and they tell us there are occupations that are
interesting, romantic, and creative—actors, writers, scientists,
physicians in scientific research institutes and in the big
clinics, and so forth—and there are professions that one acquires because one has to earn a living, where people work
their hours for the sake of money: truck drivers, assembly
line workers, janitors, salesgirls, and so on. You're not going
to maintain that even the profession of janitor has its glamorous aspect, and that we have only to discover these wonderful janitors.

There's no need to turn everything upside down and assert that the main thing is to discover your inclinations. No, the main thing is to get into the institute and make your way to the interesting and creative professions, to lift yourself out of the mass of people who work in order to live and into the group that lives in order to work.

Here are some of the comments from readers on Levinov's letter.

[From a girl about to graduate from high school:] The question he raises is worrisome to me because I am one of those millions who are graduating from school this year and whom Levinov is talking about.

In school we had a debate on the subject of "Your Dream." There were heated arguments. People talked about the meaning of one's profession in life and about how to make your dream come true. One girl, after quietly listening to our arguments, suddenly said a few words that made many people stop and think. "I want to go to any institution of higher learning, just so that I can be in a student environment and, in general, so I can have a higher education."

Silence fell on the room. I felt I knew what people were thinking. These thoughts have been pursuing me too, of late. What if I don't get into the place that I dream of going to. What'll I do? Lose one year or even more? Try and get into an institute where the competition is less? But then, how do I tally this with our conversations about the meaning of one's profession, about what is romantic and noble? —Galya Levitskaya, City of Dnepropetrovsk

[From a nineteen-year-old girl whose job is to travel around the country inspecting new machinery to be sure that it is properly installed and adjusted for operation:] Now about the romance of work.

It most often accompanies difficulties. In my view, the

romantic is first of all the unusual. You find it where things are really back-breaking, where you have to make an effort, where you have to endure.

When you stagger from one hotel to another looking for a room, when you ride on the train illegally because you weren't able to get a ticket, when you go for five days without sleep, sustaining yourself only on black coffee, anecdotes from the lives of "adjusters," and tape recordings—at times like that you somehow don't think about the "romantic and exciting." Here the formula breaks down, the state inspection commission is about to come and things are not working right—there's no romance about that! You do your job and sometimes what is not your job besides—in short, what has to be done.

And then later, at home, when you've returned to the warmth and the television set and the bathtub (you spend two hours soaking yourself), you recall everything that happened and you say to yourself, that *was* the "romance" that people talk and write about so much. You live for a week in quiet, with meals at home and all the elements of civilization, and once again you are irresistibly drawn to the unstructured life of traveling on the job.—Nina Motorina, technician-adjuster, Moscow region

"YOU COULD HAVE

BECOME AN ENGINEER"

A man in his middle-to-late twenties writes with feeling about the disdain that many people have for the workers' occupations and for the service trades. His letter appeared in Komsomolskaya pravda (Young Communist League Truth) *in December 21, 1965.*

What brought on this letter was a recent meeting with my schoolteacher. We had not seen one another for twelve years since the time I graduated from the seven-year school. All these years I have kept my feelings of warmth and gratitude toward her. And now I was glad to see her. There were the usual questions that people ask at such meetings, "How are you? What are you doing?"

How am I? Just fine. What am I doing? I'm a metal worker. I can feel my teacher's mood turn gloomy. "But you had such great ability. You could have become an engineer." After this the conversation flagged. I don't hold it against her—not at all. But the encounter set me to thinking.

There are children playing in the little square, and standing out among them is a group of young ones discussing their own affairs. I listen in. One robust little fellow with blond hair declares proudly, "My daddy is a commanding officer." Another boy says, "My daddy is a shop manager in the factory." A little girl says with a small squeal, "Well, my papa is a pilot." A thin boy about six years old says nothing. I know his father. He works in the grocery store by the Nikitin Gate.

I get up from the bench and walk along the square. Several grandmothers are sitting at a table that is rooted to the ground under a poplar tree. I hear the following: "My daughter-in-law graduates from the institute this year." Another one says, "My grandson has entered the Moscow Aviation Institute. With luck, he will get ahead in the world."

To get ahead in life. It seems to me that nowadays, for some people, this means only one thing—to get a college degree.

You may wonder why I'm writing about this. After all, it is a good thing when people take pride in the achievements of their loved ones, when youngsters are proud of their parents and grandmothers of their children and grandchildren. I agree. But why does that little boy say nothing, the one whose father works in the grocery store? And why isn't some grandmother quick to say with pride, "My grandson is a truck driver—he drives a MAZ [Moscow Automobile Plant truck]." Why did the conversation with my teacher become painful for me?

At the end of high school some boys and girls, who have never done any manual work and never really examined their own desires, are motivated by the sole wish "to get ahead in the world" and try at all costs to get into an institute, often any institute. Those with definite ability manage to get in, and after a few years the society receives a person with a degree—not a specialist, however, but a careerist. For this person the main thing, as before, is "to get ahead in the world."

In many families the parents would not even dream of having their offspring go to work in a factory and wear a worker's overalls. Not under any circumstances! The only place for him is the university. They do not take into account either the abilities or the inclinations of the young people. And if, in spite of everything, their child does not get into college, the parents take it as a tragedy.

It is understandable that a person with a degree has a higher position in any enterprise. But does a good well-qualified worker enjoy any less respect? On the job, of course, he is respected more than a mediocre administrator is.

A person can find his place in life not only in an office and at a design board, but behind the wheel of a truck and in the cab of a turret crane as well, on the scaffolding of a new building and even at a shoemaker's bench. To get ahead in the world, in my view, means primarily to win the respect of the society by the work you do and by your conduct.

I am interested to know what other readers think about this.—N. Vikhrov, metal worker, Moscow.

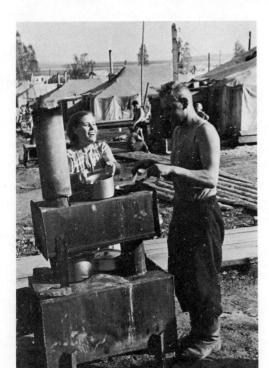

A pioneering spirit takes some young people to the new construction sites in Siberia.

(*Novosti*)

GLOSSARY

Bashmaki   shoes or low boots; an old word not often used nowadays

Brigade   widely used to indicate a work crew in Soviet industry, agriculture, construction, or transportation

Centner   a unit of weight generally equal to 50 kilograms, or 110.23 pounds; in the Soviet Union, the unit used is the metric or double centner, which equals 100 kilograms, or 220.46 pounds

Chinovnik   a petty official in Tsarist Russia; now often used in a derogatory sense

Cult of the individual   a term referring to the universal worship of Stalin, hence Stalinism

Dacha   a vacation house or cottage in the country

Druzhinnik   a member of a *druzhina*, a citizen volunteer police squad, usually recruited from the Komsomol, the Young Communist League

Great Patriotic War   the name given in the Soviet Union to World War II, to strengthen feelings of patriotism among the Soviet people

KGB   Komitet gosudarstvennoi bezopasnosti, the Committee on State Security, the formal title of the secret police

Kolkhoz   collective farm, the predominant form of organization in Soviet agriculture; there also exists the *sovkhoz*, or state farm, which is operated like an agricultural factory

Komsomol   acronym for Kommunisticheskii soiuz molodezhi, Communist Union of Youth, known as the Young

Communist League, the Party-sponsored organization for youth from their late teens through mid-twenties

Kopek the unit of currency worth a hundredth part of a ruble; at the established rate of exchange worth slightly more than one U.S. penny

Kremlin a word of Tatar origin meaning the citadel or fortress of the city, generally used to refer to the ancient fortress in Moscow, which houses churches, museums, auditoriums, theaters, and some government offices

Militiaman one who performs the functions ordinarily provided by a city policeman in the United States, such as regulating traffic or keeping public order

Obkom acronym for *oblastnoi komitet,* provincial committee of the Party or Komsomol. (The Party is organized hierarchically, beginning with the smallest unit, the cell, up through the village or city, the district, the province, and on up to the highest level.)

Okhranniki agents of the Okhrana, the political secret police in Tsarist Russia; now sometimes used to indicate overzealous guardians of dogma

Personal plot a small piece of land assigned to an individual for his own private cultivation (He may do what he wishes with the produce. The productivity has generally been much higher on private plots than in other sectors of Soviet agriculture.)

Pioneers a Party-sponsored organization for children from nine to fourteen, which organizes civic activities, recreation, and summer camps and inculcates in its members a spirit of loyalty to the Communist Party

Polytekhnikum a technical middle school offering a range of specialties

Raznochintsy literally, "from different ranks"—people from ranks, or estates, other than the gentry in nineteenth-century Russian society, particularly the nongentry intellectuals

Ruble the Russian unit of currency, presently evaluated by the Soviet Union as equivalent to $1.11

Samizdat literally, "self-publication"—writings not officially authorized for publication that are circulated privately in manuscript form

Smerdiakov a character in Dostoyevsky's novel *The Brothers Karamazov* who stands for all the bad qualities in human nature

Soviet literally, council; originally a revolutionary assemblage, later the basic legislative unit of government, whose deputies are elected (The Supreme Soviet consists of two bodies: the Council of Nationalities, elected on a proportional basis, and the Council of Union, which has representatives from each of the republics.)

Subbotnik a Saturday declared by the government as a day of voluntary labor, a tradition going back to the time of civil war immediately after the Bolshevik Revolution of 1917

Virgin Lands vast areas in Siberia and Central Asia opened up for cultivation in a large-scale campaign by Khrushchev to ease the agricultural shortages caused by low productivity in the western parts of the Soviet Union

Voskresnik the same as a *subbotnik*, except that the day set aside for work is a Sunday

White night a phenomenon occurring in northern latitudes where the days in June are so long that the sun barely sets before it rises again and where, during the brief interval of night, the sky is filled with a pale, eerie light

Workday a unit for measuring each collective farm member's contribution to the farm's production, according to which he is paid out of the farm's surplus produce or cash income

YAK-18 a training plane, named for its designer, A. S. Yakovlyev

SUGGESTIONS FOR FURTHER READING

BLAKE, PATRICIA, and MAX HAYWARD, editors. *Halfway to the Moon*. New York: Anchor Books, Doubleday & Company, 1965.

BLAKE, PATRICIA, and MAX HAYWARD, editors. *Antiworlds and "The Fifth Ace," Poetry by Andrei Voznesensky*. New York: Anchor Books, Doubleday & Company, 1967.

BRUMBERG, ABRAHAM, editor. *In Quest of Justice: Protest and Dissent in the Soviet Union Today*. New York: Praeger Publishers, 1970.

HAUTZIG, ESTHER. *The Endless Steppe: Growing Up in Siberia*. New York: Thomas Y. Crowell Company, 1968.

KAZAKOV, YURI. *Going to Town and Other Stories*. Compiled and translated by GABRIELLA AZRAEL. Boston: Houghton Mifflin Company, 1964.

MILLER, WRIGHT. *Russians as People*. New York: E. P. Dutton & Company, 1961.

NETTL, J. P. *The Soviet Achievement*. New York: Harcourt Brace Jovanovich, 1968.

REAVEY, GEORGE, editor and translator. *The New Russian Poets, 1953 to 1966: An Anthology*. New York: October House, 1966.

REDDAWAY, PETER, editor. *Underground Russia*. New York: Cowles Book Company, 1971.

SALISBURY, HARRISON E., editor. *The Soviet Union: The Fifty Years*. New York: Harcourt Brace Jovanovich, 1968.

SOLZHENITSYN, ALEXANDER I. *The First Circle*. New York and Evanston, Ill.: Harper & Row, 1968.

SOLZHENITSYN, ALEXANDER. *One Day in the Life of Ivan Denisovich*. New York: Praeger Publishers, 1963.

INDEX

Adult-youth relationship, *see* Youth-adult relationship
Agranovsky, Anatoly, 230
Agranovsky, Valery, 85
Agriculture, 157; *see also* Collective farms
Akhmadulina, Bella, 170
Amalrik, Andrei, 25, 37
Ambitions, 269–75; results of, 271–74; of students, 272–73; of workers, 271–74; of youth, 57, 60
Army, 18; discipline in, 209–12; and literature, 213–15; *see also* Military service
Arts, 66, 68, 146, 236–42

Baltic republics, 60
Birth control methods, 177, 179–80
Bolshevik Revolution, *see* Russian Revolution
Building management, 230–32
Bukovsky, Vladimir, 252–58, 262–63

Censorship, 54–55, 240–43, 244, 246–67
Children, 41–42; problems with, 188–91; unwanted, 182–83
China, 38, 49–50
Churches, restoration of, 137–41
City life *vs.* country life, 118–22
City youth, 43–70; education of, 46–47; ideals of, 45; *see also* Youth
Collective farms, 9–11, 19–26; chairmen of, 10, 23–24, 26; earnings on, 14; education on, 21; management of, 23; marriage on, 40–41, 152; problems of, 21–24, 25–26
Committee on State Security (KGB), 249–51, 253–54, 258, 259–61
Communist Party, United States, 257

Communist Party of the Soviet Union (CPSU), 37–38
Constitution of U.S.S.R., 255–56
Consumer goods, 228–29
Councils of government ("Soviets"), 57
Country life, 2–14, 131–36; *vs.* city life, 118–22; Vladimir region, 2–8; *see also* Village life
Country youth, 4–7; education of, 12–14; migration of, 11, 15–18; and World War II, 7–8; *see also* Youth
CPSU, *see* Communist Party of the Soviet Union
Crime and Punishment (Dostoyevsky), 123–28
Criminal Code, 255–56; revision of, 252
Criticism, 227–43
Culture, 48; and clubs, 27–36; workers' interests in, 233–35
Czechoslovakia, invasion of, 51, 59, 247

Damansky Island, 49, 223–25
Daniel, Larisa, 262–63
De-Stalinization, 65–66
Delone, Vadim, 252
Derzhavin, Gavril Romanovich, 278–81
Dickens, Charles, 128
Dissent, 244–67
Dorosh, Yefim, 142
Dostoyevsky, Andrei Fyodorovich, 123, 124
Dostoyevsky, Fyodor, 123–28

Economy, criticism of, 228–29

Education, 16, 42, 52–53, 58, 59, 61, 68, 88, 269–95; of city youth, 46–47; of country youth, 12–14; "dropouts" from, 20; and environment, 280–81, 291–93; patriotism in, 204–5; political, 37–39; and preparation for university, 282–85; sex, 181
Endless Steppe, The: Growing Up in Siberia (Hautzig), 129

"Fifteen Boys" (Akhmadulina), 170–71
Foreign relations: with China, 38, 49–50; with France, 106; with United States, 38, 50, 200–201; with West, 246; with West Germany, 203
France, 106

Gagarin, Yuri, 67
Galich, Alexander, 76, 245
Generation gap, *see* Youth-adult relationship
Gogol, Nikolai, 53
Going to Town and Other Stories (Kazakov), 130–36
Gorky, university at, 85–89
Granin, Daniil, 123
"Grievance, The" (Soloukhin), 2–7
Grigoryev, E., 91

Hautzig, Esther, 129
Heroes of young people, 67
"Hippies," 174–75

"I Am Goya" (Voznesensky), 199
In Quest of Justice (Brumberg), 252–58, 259–61, 262–63, 267
"Incident on Mamai Hill" (Nekrasov), 218–22
Involuntary Journey to Siberia (Amalrik), 25–26, 37–39

Kassil, Lev, 172
Kautmann, František, 123, 128
Kazakov, Yuri, 130
KGB, *see* Committee on State Security
Khrushchev, Nikita S., 66

Kochetov, Vsevolod, 202
Kolkhoz, see Collective farms
Komsomol (Young Communist League), 33, 58–59, 67–68, 250; and student problems, 192
Korchagin, Pavel, 67
Korean War, 39
Kostroma experiment, 21–22
Kostyashkin, E., 181
Kremlin (Rostov), 142–43
Kushev, Yevgeny, 252

Legal cases, 296–314
Lenin, Vladimir I., 22, 66
Leningrad, 123–28
Literature, 53–54, 59, 61, 66–67, 129, 236–39; and army, 214–15; on war, 67, 206–12, 217
Litvinov, Pavel, 259–61; criticism of, 264–66; support of, 262–63
Lyapino, village of, 9–10

Makarenko, Anton, 60, 68–69
Manners, 159–72; of youth, 161–70
Mao Tse-tung, 39, 49
Marriage, 48, 57, 181–82; on collective farms, 40–41, 152; and peasants, 148–57; problems of, 186–96; results of, 186–96; and students, 186–93
Material possessions, 71–77; and comforts, 76; corrupting influence of, 73–75; of students, 85–89
May Day, 56
Merkulov, S., 167
Military service, 18, 50–51; *see also* Army
Monasteries, 137–41
Morals, 56–57, 62, 159–60, 172–96; and Russian Revolution, 159–60; and World War II, 159–60
Music, 47, 56, 61–62, 68, 72, 245

Nekrasov, Viktor, 206, 218
Night of the Nightingales, The (Yezhov), 209
Northern Song (Popkov), 146, 147
Nudity in art, 184–85
Nurseries, 190–91

Pacifism, 197–225
Patriotism, 197–225
Peasants, 14, 19–26, 82–84, 146–57
Periodicals, 54; "underground," 252, 262
Phoenix '66, 256, 266
Pioneers (children's organization), 67
Professions, choice of, 286–90
Protest movement, 252; criticism of, 264–66

Radio, 54
Rieder, Adolf, 11
Rostov, Yaroslavl Province, 142–45
Rozov, Viktor, 243
Russia, 142–47; *see also* Union of Soviet Socialist Republics
Russian Revolution (1917), 53; goals of, 71; and morals, 159–60

Saint Petersburg, *see* Leningrad
Schools, *see* Education
"Second Night, The" (Nekrasov), 206–8
Sex, *see* Morals
Sex education, 181
Siberia, 37–39, 45, 129; life in, 27–30, 130–36; travel in, 60, 61; Virgin Lands in, 223–24
Simonov, Konstantin, 216
Smolensk Province, 11
Soloukhin, Vladimir, 2
Solovetsky Islands, 137–41
Songs, "underground," 245; *see also* Music
Soviets (councils of government), 57
Stalin, Joseph, 40, 66, 216–17
Stalingrad, 219–21
Students, 137–41; ambitions of, 272–73; arrests of, 248–51; clothing of, 86–87; housing of, 192; income of, 87–88; marriages of, 186–93; material possessions of, 85–89; stipends for, 87–88; and support of Bukovsky, 262–63; and travel, 85–86; and university, 282–85; and vocations, 89

Three Days in the Life of Viktor Chernyshev (Grigoryev), 91–116

Totma District, 14
Travel, 56, 60, 61; and youth, 145

"Underground" publications, 252, 262
Union of Soviet Socialist Republics: and China, 38, 49–50; Constitution of, 255–56; and France, 106; isolation of, from West, 246; and United States, 38, 50, 200–201; and West Germany, 203; *see also* Russia
United States: Communist Party of, 257; and U.S.S.R., 38, 50, 200–201
University admissions, 282–85; *see also* Students

Vakhmin, Vyacheslav, 248–49
Vietnam, 38
Village life: conditions of, 12–14; and education, 12–14; *see also* Country life
"Village" writers, 118
Virgin Lands, 223–24; *see also* Siberia
Vladimir region, 2, 4–5
Vocations, 269–93
Vologda Province, 14
Voronezh region, 12
Voznesensky, Andrei, 63, 199
Vysotsky, V., 201

"Walk in Dostoyevsky's City, A" (Granin), 123–28
West: external relations with, 246; isolation from, 246
West Germany and U.S.S.R., 203
What Is It You Want? (Kochetov), 202
Women, 18, 146, 147; role of, 18, 41, 48, 57, 165–69, 178–80, 186–96, 272–74, 280–82
Workers: ambitions of, 271–74; in construction, 275–77; cultural interests of, 233–35; education of, 369, 283–85; life of, 91–116
World War II, 7–8, 197, 216–17; and morals, 59–60

Yakhimovich, Ivan, 267
Yanov, Alexander, 19
Yashin, Alexander, 118
Yezhov, Valentin, 206
Young Communist League, *see* Komsomol
Young People: About Themselves and Their Contemporaries, 278–80
Youth, 1–69, 146–47; ambitions of, 57, 60; amusements of, 55; attitudes of, 78–84, 197, 223–25; city, 43–69, 80–82; country, 4–8, 11, 15–18; criticism by, 228–29; girls, 56–57; goals of, 78–84; ideals of, 45, 53; independent development of, 69; interests of, 64; manners of, 161–70; material desires of, 71–72; migration of, 1–2, 19–20; and politics, 54–55; protests of, 54–55; and travel, 145; Western, 67
Youth-adult relationship, 16–17, 24, 46, 62, 66, 79, 193–94, 218, 243
Yunost (Youth), letters to, 54, 59, 286–90